WHY IS THIS
HAPPENING TO ME?

WHY IS THIS HAPPENING TO ME?

HOW TO TRUST IN GOD'S PLAN WHEN YOUR WORLD IS FALLING APART

GINA TRONCO

ethos
collective

Printed in the United States of America

Published by Ethos Collective™
PO Box 43, Powell, OH 43065
www.ethoscollective.vip

LCCN: 2023905498
ISBN: 978-1-63680-152-0 (paperback)
ISBN: 978-1-63680-153-7 (hardback)
ISBN: 978-1-63680-154-4 (ebook)

Available in paperback, hardback, e-book, and audiobook

All Scripture quotations, unless otherwise indicated, are taken from
the Holy Bible, New International Version®, NIV®. Copyright © 1973,
1978, 1984 by Biblica, Inc.TM Used by permission of Zondervan.
All rights reserved worldwide.

Any Internet addresses (websites, blogs, etc.) and telephone numbers
printed in this book are offered as a resource. They are not intended in
any way to be or imply an endorsement by Ethos Collective™, nor does
Ethos Collective™ vouch for the content of these sites and numbers for
the life of this book.

To my strong, independent daughters—Julia, Isabella, and Olivia—who kept me going through the hard times. When life seemed too overwhelming, your smiles were a reminder that there was still hope.

Table of Contents

Foreword

If you've heard my story, then you know how I've experienced pain and betrayal. To experience ultimate healing, I needed to learn forgiveness and grace in brand-new ways. These lessons aren't always easy or welcomed, and I share them in *Your Secret Name*.

Gina Tronco echoes my sentiment. Without asking, she experienced pain and betrayal too. In her darkest days, she caused headaches and heartaches.

In times of trial, it's easy to cry out to the heavens and ask, "Why?"

Jesus knows how we feel. On the cross, he cried out to his Father, "Why?" Although there was no audible reply or detailed rationale, after his darkest day, Jesus experienced a resurrection.

Gina is also proof we can overcome, even when we wonder, *Why is This Happening to Me?* Her story will bring you hope and encouragement. She shares every detail, beginning with her upbringing in a working-class Italian family. Her love story seemed destined for a fairy tale ending. But life had a different plan in store for her, and her perfect life began falling apart without any warning.

In the midst of the chaos, Gina turned to God and discovered a supernatural strength. Her story is one of resilience, perseverance, and faith. Brace yourself for an emotional rollercoaster as you dive into the pages of Gina's book and witness her journey through infidelity, separation, and a cancer diagnosis in just a few short months.

When your world falls apart, God isn't surprised or overwhelmed. He's committed to never leave you or forsake you. Gina's life is an example of how God will hold you close and walk with you even on your darkest days.

—Kary Oberbrunner,
Wall Street Journal and *USA Today* bestselling author of
12 books, CEO of Igniting Souls

Prologue

"Bienvenidos a México, familia Tronco!" said the concierge who greeted us at the entrance of the Fairmont Mayakoba Resort in Cancún.

This was the start of our family vacation celebrating our eldest daughter, Julia's, sixteenth birthday. Julia had chosen the exotic location, and my husband, Alex, and I gladly fulfilled her wish.

Our concierge, Roberto, offered to escort us to our connecting rooms—one for our three daughters, Julia, Bella, and Olivia, and one for Alex and me—and we all followed him, eager to start celebrating our special event. As Roberto opened the door, the dazzling floral smell of dahlias—Mexico's national flower—which decorated the room welcomed us.

"Gina," Alex called to me. "You should come and see our bedroom!"

After taking a moment to watch my daughters' delight in their room, I stepped through the adjoining door to join my husband. "Wow, this is gorgeous!" I said, feeling as much awe as my daughters showed with their room.

My eyes moved around the room, marveling at the large king-size bed that led to a beautiful en-suite bathroom with two sinks and a soak-in tub, complete with a wooden tray placed at the end of it. But the most breathtaking feature was the view of the beach and the sea with the July sun kissing the water, making it glitter as if it were made of thousands of small diamonds.

Before we arrived, I called the hotel and had them prepare a birthday cake for Julia's big day. It was her favorite: vanilla cake with Boston cream and fresh cut-up strawberries.

"Julia," Alex called. "Close your eyes. We have a surprise for you!"

Alex and I walked into the girls' room, holding her birthday cake with two candles—for the number sixteen—lit and ready to be blown.

"Happy birthday to you," her two sisters, Bella and Olivia, sang in unison as Alex and I joined them. "Happy birthday to you, happy birthday, dear Julia . . ." she slowly opened her eyes and, with raised eyebrows and slightly parted lips that echoed her gasp of surprise, paused on every detail of the cake decorations as if to visually savor it. Then, she came closer to the candles, closed her eyes to make her wish, and blew over them—our clue to finish singing the song. "Happy birthday to you!"

As everyone clapped, I felt my eyes getting wet as tears filled with memories of my once-little girl cuddling with her teddy bear overtook me. And now there she was, on her sixteenth birthday, looking like a beautiful young woman.

"Mom's crying," Julia said with a smirk.

And the rest of the family proceeded to make fun of me for being such a softy. I shook my head at the mockery, letting out a sigh of exasperation.

"So, what would you girls like to do?" Alex asked, ever the caring and attentive father.

"Let's go to the beach!" Bella said.

"Yeah, I need to work on my tan," Olivia chimed in.

"Okay, meet you there!" I said. After taking another moment to enjoy the sight of my three young ladies, I returned to our bedroom to change.

Now, what should I wear? I pondered as I started looking through the suitcase Alex had placed on the bed. "So many choices," I joked as I looked through my sundresses, deciding which one I was in the mood to wear. *Perfect!* I thought as I unfolded my burgundy crochet dress that went well with my charcoal gray bathing suit. After adding the finishing touches—my sunhat, an application of raspberry chapstick to protect my lips from the heat, and my flip-flops—I walked with Alex through the resort toward the beach.

The open space concept of the resort offered breathtaking views of the crystal-clear waters of the Caribbean Sea that, along with the luscious and vibrant green of the tropical forest, beautifully framed the vast shoreline and its white sand. Bamboo tiki bars created a fun and exotic atmosphere, showcasing colorful drinks that looked similar to the ones we were given upon arrival and took with us to drink at the beach. Cozy white couches and comfortable teal loveseats faced the open veranda and invited guests to sit, relax, and enjoy the live music show with its signature wooden conga drums, whose sound captivated your senses and made your hips follow the rhythm.

"The gym is to the left," Alex said. "We'll go there in the morning as usual?"

I nodded. Alex and I enjoyed working out together, and while on vacation, we always made sure to keep up with our fitness routine.

"Oh look, there they are!" Alex said, pointing to our three daughters, already lounging on the beach. (I must've taken longer to get ready than I thought.)

"Hello there," I offered my greeting, which was reciprocated with a slight handwave in true teenage girls' fashion.

"They are playing drums out there on the veranda. You should go dance," I teased them.

"Oh. Em. Gee!" Olivia, our youngest, said, sounding rather monotone. She had her Ray-Ban sunglasses on, but I felt her rolling her eyes at me.

With an amused chuckle, I shrugged and joined Alex on the lounge chairs he'd secured. The light, warm breeze from the sea brought an aftertaste of salt water to my lips, which I enjoyed as I always associated the ocean smell with vacation mode. The feeling of bliss filled me and amplified as Alex reached for my hand, squeezed it, and smiled at me when I looked at him.

That evening, after enjoying a delicious dinner on the beach, surrounded by tiki torches that created an intimate and soft ambiance, the girls went to the resort's club. Tired from a wonderful but long day, Alex and I walked back to our room, accompanied by the starry night and the sound of the waves gently crashing on the shore.

"Oh yeah? I want to see *you* do Romanian deadlifts!" I told the girls. I was sweaty from spending an hour at the gym with Alex, and they were teasing me as usual.

"Sure, let's do it!" Olivia said, grabbing an invisible bar.

"No, no, no," I admonished her. "You hurt yourself if you do it that way." Then, I began demonstrating with the same invisible bar. "First of all, you have to use an overhand grip to hold the bar. Then, you have to pull the bar at hip level, shoulders and back straight, and push your hips back to slowly lower the bar. Then—"

"Okay, Mom, we get it," Olivia interrupted me. "You know better."

I winked at her.

"We'll see you girls at breakfast in about fifteen minutes," Alex told the girls as he accompanied them outside.

Fifteen minutes. I better check what time it is now, I thought and grabbed my phone, which was sitting on my nightstand. I turned on the screen, and the date and time on my phone read: *July 3, 2017, 8:58 a.m.*

But instead of my screen wallpaper, a photo of our family, I found my Facebook page open.

A photo immediately caught my attention.

It was a photo of him. Alex. My husband. With a much younger woman.

Words. There are words describing this photo.

We have been together . . . is all I remember reading.

"Honey?" Alex recalled my attention.

I dropped the phone on the bed.

"I . . ." I tried to speak, but the words died in my throat.

Alex glanced at the phone and saw the photo. He picked it up quickly and deleted it.

"It's not what you think," I heard him say, but his words weren't registering. "She's . . ." He didn't know how to continue the sentence and left it to hang in midair.

Almost three decades of my unconditional love for him was gone in a flash.

I looked at the phone he placed back in my hand and then at him but couldn't utter a single word. All I saw in front of me was almost three decades of my unconditional love for him gone in a flash. Our marriage, which everybody described as perfect, collapsed like a sandcastle, shattering into thousands of grains of sand, carried away into the abyss by the unforgiving water.

Alex is having an affair.

PART ONE
Living a Blessed Life

Chapter One

March of 1990 was an unusually warm month for Albany, with temperatures reaching well into the 70s. Many of my high school friends were enjoying the early spring weather by going out more often and spending more time together. But not me. As usual, rain or shine, I had to work at my family's deli right after I was done with school—and on weekends.

And I hated every single minute of it, of course, because as a teenager, having to be at the deli from three o'clock in the afternoon until ten o'clock at night when we closed was not in the top ten things I wanted to do. Fortunately for me, however, my parents were kind enough not to force me to go to the deli when I had cheer practice three times a week after school. Whenever I complained about having to work at the deli, my mom and dad reminded me to be thankful, and I was lucky to spend so much time with both of them while getting paid for it.

"Gina, this is what we do in our family," my dad would say, raising his chin with pride.

"I know, Pa, I know," I would reassure him, doing my best to hide the fact that my eyes rolled every time he said that.

My dad was born and raised in Calabria, southern Italy, and moved to New York in 1966, whereas my mother was born in the United States but also had a solid Italian heritage—my maternal grandparents were from the region of Campania, also southern Italy. They often told me stories of how their parents—my grandparents—grew up during World War II and had nothing to eat for many days. They were poor and barely had a third-grade education because, during those times, going to school was a luxury most could not afford. In order to survive, my grandparents had to work from a very early age to bring in as much money as they possibly could so the family could stay afloat. Their intense work ethic was clearly absorbed by my parents, who worked hard their entire life.

However, my parents also stressed the importance of education, especially my mother, who often told me, "Three things in life are inevitable: taxes, college, and death." Meaning I had no choice but to go to college—which didn't seem like a punishment because I wanted to pursue higher education. I often think the reason she insisted so much on me going to college was because my grandparents did not allow her to attend college because she was a woman—male children pursued an education, while female children had to stay home and learn how to be great homemakers. Still, having to always go to work at the deli caused me many heavy sighs and much eye-rolling.

Fortunately, my monotonous routine got an upgrade when a tall, dark, and handsome Italian boy literally came knocking on my door one late afternoon. I was trying to quickly finish my homework before going to the deli and was immersed in my reading when I received this unexpected visitor.

"Hi," he said before pausing a bit too long for comfort.

"Hello," I replied, waiting for him to break the slightly awkward silence.

"Um . . ." He shook his head as if to get rid of the sudden daze he had fallen into and then added, "I am collecting money for the Super Dance to raise awareness for muscular dystrophy."

He sounded as though he had said that all in one breath, rather rehearsed.

"Oh, I'm sorry, but my parents aren't home at the moment." He was so good-looking, and I really wanted to help the cause—I had heard about the Super Dance at school, which started at seven o'clock in the evening and lasted through the night until seven o'clock in the morning. My brain went into overdrive. If he was raising money for it, then it meant we attended the same high school! "I'm sorry," I apologized again, wishing I had something better to say.

"It's okay," he said, offering a shy smile. "Thanks anyway!"

I stood in the doorway for a moment, watching him walk away. As I started to close the door, he spun around and quickly asked, "Are you going to the Super Dance?"

My cheeks felt like they were on fire. Of course, I wasn't going—I had yet to receive an invitation. I didn't know what to say—*Should I lie and say that I was going, or should I just tell him the truth and look like a little girl?* My parents taught me not to lie, but my pride wouldn't let me tell the truth either. So, I simply shook my head no and closed the door.

5

A few days later, at school, I overheard a few girls in the hall saying that some guy named Alex was back from Italy. Apparently, they were all excited about it. Then, during cheer practice, a girlfriend of mine asked me if I had heard the news.

"Yes, but I have no clue who he is," I explained without thinking too much about it.

"Oh my goodness, he is the most handsome guy!" she said, clapping her hands excitedly. "He is tall and so dreamy! Plus, he speaks Italian, which sounds sooo exotic and romantic!"

He speaks Italian, huh? Big deal; so does my family! I shrugged and refocused on cheer practice.

That afternoon, while I was completing my homework, the phone rang. Once again, I was alone—my parents had been working at the deli for hours as usual—so it was up to me to answer it.

"Hello?" I said absentmindedly while glancing over at the math exercise that was turning out to be a bigger pain than I thought it would be.

"Yes, may I speak with Gina, please?" asked the male voice on the other line.

"Um, this is she." *Who's calling me?*

"Hi, Gina," he said, his tone slightly upbeat. "This is Fred from school."

"Fred?" I said, unsure as to who he was.

"Yep, from Mr. Klein's class," he specified.

Oh, our English teacher!

"How have you been?" he asked.

"Come on, ask her . . ." urged another male voice in the background.

What was going on? And why was Fred calling me?

He must have sensed my unease through my silence and quickly added, "I'm calling because my friend Alex, who

6

recently came back from Italy, would like to invite you to go with him to the Super Dance."

"Who?" I asked. *There's that Alex name again*, I thought.

"He said he met you the other day when he came over to your house while raising money for the dance," Fred explained. "He said you were home alone and couldn't offer any money—"

"Oh yes!" I interrupted him so quickly that I surprised even myself.

"'Yes,' you remember him, or 'yes,' you'd like to accept his invite?"

Shoot, what do I say now? He was really good-looking, and I couldn't believe that I had indeed met the famous "just back from Italy" Alex.

"I have to ask my parents, but I'd love to," I replied. I suddenly felt my index finger had fallen asleep, which was how I realized that I had been twirling the phone cord around it so tightly that I almost stopped the blood from circulating.

"Okay, great," Fred said, as I overheard a *Yes!* in the background.

When we hung up, I placed both hands over my mouth, which was open in excitement. Needless to say, despite my best effort, I couldn't focus on that math problem that afternoon. So, I hurried to the deli to ask my parents for their permission to attend the school dance. After their affirmative reply, my lips curved upward into a smile that didn't leave for the entire evening.

The next day at school, Alex came over and officially introduced himself to me.

"Nice to meet you, too," I said.

"Thank you for accepting my invite to come to the dance with me tomorrow night," he said, smiling and looking down at his feet.

I was glad I wasn't the only one who felt so shy and embarrassed.

"Thank you for inviting me," I whispered, almost hoping he wouldn't hear me.

But he did, and he looked up at me. The moment our eyes met, I felt as if a lightning bolt had just rushed through my whole body. That feeling remained through the seemingly endless hours leading up to our date.

At the dance, Alex and I talked as much as we danced.

"So I heard you went back to Italy for a while?" I asked him, feeling more and more comfortable around him with every ticking minute.

"Yes," he explained. "My parents travel back and forth from Sicily for work."

"Oh, so you'll be leaving again?" I asked, trying hard not to let my sadness show but failing.

"No, I am here to stay now," Alex reassured me. "School is important to them, you know, and they want me to succeed. I'm staying with some family friends for now. Then, when my folks come back, I'll go live with them again."

The night went by in a flash, and before I knew it, the night sky was giving way to the sun; it was time to go home.

"Thank you for being my date tonight," Alex said in a low voice.

I smiled as I glanced at him, feeling my heart flutter.

"I would like it if you were my date again," he whispered, holding my hand. "Would you like to go out for ice cream sometime?"

I nodded yes and tilted my head to the side, hoping the faint light from the rising sun wasn't bright enough to reveal just how red my cheeks had gotten.

That night was the first date of many. Alex and I spent as much time together as possible: he started working at my parents' deli, and we went to Friendly's for ice cream every Friday night. My mom and dad welcomed him into the family as if he was their own son and, in typical Italian fashion, always gave him way more pasta than me because, "He's a boy, and he needs to grow up big and strong!" We couldn't be home alone without my parents, so the only time we were allowed to be unchaperoned was when we went to the movies or out for ice cream—although Alex often made sure to point out that it wasn't as good as Sicilian gelato.

Like many young couples, we broke up a couple of times, but it was never for longer than a few days, and we always found our way back to one another. Yes, we were young, but we clicked from the very beginning. It helped that we shared important values, including how much we cared about our education. Alex had big dreams, and even though he didn't always have his parents nearby, he was determined to make them proud by achieving everything he had set his mind to. Much like me, he came from a humble family who couldn't afford their wants and, at times, couldn't afford their needs either, but they were rich at heart because they had each other and their faith.

They were rich at heart because they had each other and their faith.

After high school, I attended college to study music, which had always been a passion of mine. I started playing the piano in second grade, inspired by my family members who played several instruments, even though they could not read music. Still, they were so good that they were in various bands and often played at weddings and other ceremonies. Of course, my college was close to my house—my parents didn't want me to be far away from them, nor did they allow me to live on campus when I was a freshman, so I always had to go back home after class and, yes, work at the deli. Alex attended a different college nearby to study business.

Upon graduating, Alex immediately got a job at Northwestern Mutual, a financial services company, and I was happy to have been hired as a music teacher at a local school. Our relationship grew stronger and more solid throughout the years, but we still could not be left home alone, even though we were both in our early twenties. That all changed one Friday night on June 20, 1997, when I returned home from working at the deli and found Alex there with my mother.

"Hey," I said as soon as I saw him. "What are you doing here?"

"Oh, I just came to see you," Alex said, but his tone indicated something was up. He seemed restless with his hands as if trying hard to keep his composure. "You going to take a shower?"

"Do I smell that bad?" We both laughed. "Yes, I'll go shower."

"Alright, I'm on my way out then," my mom said out of nowhere. My dad was still at the deli, which meant Alex and I would be alone in the house. *What's going on here?* I thought but didn't voice it.

After my shower, I got dressed and walked out of the room when . . . I saw a path of rose petals through the hall, leading to the kitchen. My heart started beating faster and faster as I brought my hands over my mouth. *Could this be?* I tiptoed through the petals and reached the kitchen, where I saw him on one knee, looking up at me, his hands trembling with emotion, holding a small open box containing a beautiful and shiny diamond ring.

"Gina," he whispered. "Will you marry me?"

We had been together for seven years, so getting married felt like the next natural step. Still, I was overcome by surprise and excitement. Having lost the ability to speak, I simply nodded my head yes. The moment felt as powerful as the first time we looked into each other's eyes. Alex effortlessly rose and placed the ring on my finger. As soon as the band settled into place, I thrust my arms around his neck and started daydreaming about bridal gowns, bouquets, and wedding cakes.

Our lips met, sealing our future with a kiss, when I suddenly broke off and said, "Wait, my parents!" My excitement turned to panic, and my eyes darted around the room for a glass of water to quench my sudden parchment.

"They know," Alex reassured me with a smile. "I asked for your hand in marriage, and your father approved."

I was happy to hear he had first asked my parents' permission and that they had given him their blessing.

That evening, we had a delicious celebratory dinner with our parents and siblings and began planning our wedding day. It would be held at our church, of course, and all our family and friends would be invited.

And that was how the new chapter of our life began. A chapter filled with many highs and a few devastating lows.

Chapter Two

Throughout my childhood, weekly dinners at my grandmother's house were the norm. And now that Alex and I were married, the routine certainly hadn't changed—it just meant she now had one more guest to share food with, which was no big deal, as my grandmother always believed that where there's food for three, there's food for four.

"I think I have the flu," I told Alex during one of our weekly gatherings. My head felt heavy, and all my bones felt like they were broken.

"How long have you been feeling this way?" my mom asked as she pressed her cheek against my forehead—just as she did when I was a child to check for a fever.

"A few days now," I said. "It's because of the kids at school, I'm sure." I loved teaching music at a school, but every teacher knows you are constantly sick the first two years you work at a new school because your body is apparently a magnet for every single germ that attends school along with the kids they live on.

"Why don't I take you to urgent care real quick?" my mom offered.

I looked at Alex, who nodded in agreement. He had been swamped with work lately. He was working and studying all hours of the day and well into the night because, as a young representative for the financial services company Northwestern Mutual, he had to earn his stripes in order to climb the corporate ladder.

"Alright," I said, slowly pushing my chair back from the dining room table.

I kissed Alex and my grandparents goodbye and went to urgent care with my mom.

Once there, I was relieved to see only one person in the waiting room. I sighed and took a seat, feeling as though the car ride had worsened the situation—in addition to the aches and pains, I also felt lightheaded. I don't recall how much time passed before they called back because I was so focused on not fainting. *Breathe,* I kept repeating in my head as I twisted and squeezed my hands together in my lap.

Eventually, a nurse, who looked like she'd seen her fair share of sick people that day, ushered me into the room that smelled like it had just been sterilized. Needless to say, this didn't help with my symptoms. In a clinical manner, the woman asked me about my symptoms, medical history, and if there was any chance I might be pregnant.

"Pregnant?" I said, scoffing at the idea. *How absurd,* I thought. "No, there is no way I am pregnant."

The nurse shrugged. "When was your last period, ma'am?"

Why is she insisting?

"Uhm . . ." I looked up at the ceiling squinting my eyes. *Wait, when was it?* "I don't remember, actually. It's been a while, though."

"Ma'am, I think you're pregnant," the nurse said, scribbling something down on the chart. Without any further questions, testing, or a diagnosis, she handed me discharge papers and sent me back home.

I think you're pregnant.

✝

"A pregnancy test?" Alex said in a tone that clearly conveyed his surprise at the sight of the little rectangular box. "Wait, why didn't they run a test at the clinic?"

"I don't know why . . . but she insisted so much that Mom convinced me it was worth buying it on our way back home," I said, scoffing at the absurdity. My mom had dropped me off at my house with a casual "Let me know" in addition to her usual goodbye.

I was convinced the contents of that little box would soon confirm the nurse was wrong in her assumption. After reading the instructions and taking the test, it was time to wait the three minutes that would eventually prove me right. *Couldn't the nurse have just given me some Tylenol instead?*

"Thirty seconds have gone by," Alex said, staring hard at the stick sitting on the bathroom sink as if to will it into making a decision.

You can never be completely ready to welcome children.

Alex and I had been married for about a year now, and even though we knew we wanted to have children one day, we also wanted to be a bit more prepared to welcome them. According to my mom and grandmother, though, one could never be ready

14

to welcome children. But I at least wanted Alex to have a less demanding work schedule, and I was still unsure as to whether or not a baby would mean that I would ultimately give up teaching. It wasn't an easy scenario to think through, and there were many factors to consider: most importantly, I loved my job because it provided me with a creative outlet.

I started playing piano when I was in second grade and the French horn when I was in fourth. By the time I reached high school, I had played in both the band and the orchestra. My passion for music came from my family: my grandfather was self-taught and learned how to play the mandolin, guitar, and accordion—without ever actually learning how to read music, although he clearly had an ear for it. After perfecting his skills, he taught his children. They eventually became so good that they decided to join various bands in the area.

It was natural for me to teach music, given that music had always been such a prominent part of my life. But my teacher's salary wasn't great. And while the school was close enough to my home, would it feel close with a baby to drop off at daycare?

Alex's gasp shook me back to the present. I looked at him and followed his gaze, which was still glued to the pregnancy test. *Oh dear...* My fingers trembled as I picked it up to make sure my eyes were not deceiving me.

One, two. I counted the lines that had shyly appeared on the pregnancy test.

They were faint, but there was no mistaking it: we had a baby on the way!

Half crying and half laughing, Alex and I stared at one another before he embraced me and kissed me. As our lips separated, my blurry vision found his eyes. They sparkled with tears of joy, which told me all I needed to know: we were going to be okay.

Still, somewhat in shock, we drove to my parent's house to share the good news. I was a married woman now, yet I remember feeling scared and embarrassed. How would they react? Would they be disappointed we didn't wait longer to have children? All my fears went flying out the window the moment I found the courage to tell them. My mom placed both hands over her mouth, which was open with sheer joy and surprise. My dad, just home from the deli, smiled and congratulated us on the happy announcement.

That night, as I lay down in bed next to Alex, who was already sound asleep, I gently placed my open palm on my belly and thought of the baby that would join our family in a matter of months. And as much as my head was crowded with big decisions to make and my heart filled with big feelings to sort through, I couldn't help but smile and thank God for this unexpected miracle as I drifted off to sleep.

I thanked God for this unexpected miracle.

✝

My pregnancy proceeded well, with a sonogram in the second trimester revealing we were expecting a baby girl. Alex's jaw dropped to the floor when he heard the news; he was ecstatic! Still busy with work, he felt even more motivated and driven because he knew he had a daughter on the way. Meanwhile, I left my teaching position but continued helping my parents at the deli whenever I could.

However, when I was six months pregnant, my beloved grandfather Luigi—my mother's father—passed away. My mom was the oldest of seven children, and when I was a little girl, I spent most of my free time at my grandparents' house, where I played with my uncles and aunts, who were barely ten years older than me. Nonno Luigi was a constant presence in my life: he taught me how to play an Italian card game Scopa, pinched my cheeks every time he saw me, and he doted on me, making sure his own children were not being too rough when they played with me. His death was something I felt terribly guilty for because my family had always believed that when a new life begins, another one ends. And I couldn't shake off the thought that I had basically killed him, no matter how much my husband and parents rolled their eyes whenever I expressed how I felt about his sudden passing.

What happened right after our daughter was born sealed my connection between her birth and his death. Alex

When a new life begins, another one ends.

and I were asleep in my hospital room, which, only a few hours prior, had been filled with pretty much all of our family members who had wanted to come and take part in our joyous occasion.

I was in labor for eighteen hours, so once our beautiful baby daughter was born, most of our relatives left to go back to their homes, while my parents and in-laws stayed a little longer to take in as much of their granddaughter as possible. Exhausted from a long day of big emotions, it wasn't long before Alex and I fell asleep with our brand-new baby sleeping in a small bassinet next to my bed.

Suddenly, Alex woke me up, his voice shaking and his hands trembling. My immediate reaction was to look over at our newborn, who seemed to be sleeping just fine.

"You okay?" I asked Alex, who was having a hard time catching his breath.

"He came here to see the baby," he mumbled under his breath, staring at me so intensely that I sat up instantly as a jolt of adrenaline rushed through my body. I was quickly reminded of what I had just gone through by the soreness that immediately held my body hostage.

"Who?" I asked. I was in pain and didn't know whether to feel confused or scared.

Alex sat next to me in bed, took a deep breath, and finally said, "Your grandfather."

My eyes opened wide, and I felt my heart thumping in my chest.

"I don't know what happened, but . . ." Alex ran his fingers through his hair. "I woke up suddenly and couldn't move. It was the oddest sensation because I felt like I was paralyzed. I was fully awake and conscious, but I was not in control of my body. I saw him standing over the bassinet, looking over her. He then turned to me and said, 'I just wanted to come and meet the baby.' I wanted to scream, rub my eyes to make sure I wasn't dreaming, but I couldn't move, Gina! Then he kissed her forehead and left. And that's when I was able to move and come tell you!"

He was sweating.

I, however, was crying. I knew God had sent my grandfather to meet the new child in our family.

Alex and I had gone back and forth on which name to pick for our baby, eventually opting to make the decision after we met her. But my grandfather's visit had put all other options to rest. There was only one name, the one he loved the most and used with any woman he met, regardless of what her real name actually was.

"Julia," I whispered as I looked at our soundly sleeping daughter.

Alex smiled in agreement.

Barely three days after bringing Julia home, I was already at the deli visiting and helping my parents with their workload while they got some good bonding time with the sleepy baby. By now, all our most loyal customers had heard that Julia had arrived and stopped by the deli to see her, complimenting us on having such a beautiful newborn.

While motherhood was proving to be easier than I thought, Julia had started to confuse day and night, which meant that both Alex and I were sleepless by sunrise and exhausted by sunset. It was becoming increasingly common for me to find Alex in the wee hours of the morning, sitting in his armchair with Julia asleep on his chest. But after the first few times—which I made sure to immortalize with photos that would eventually make the family album—I was worried that his performance at work would suffer from sheer exhaustion. I needed to find a solution.

"You've got to flip her," my grandmother said matter-of-factly when I told her about our struggles with Julia's sleeping schedule.

"Flip her? What does that mean?" I was beginning to wonder if I was so tired that I could no longer comprehend my native language.

"Yes, my mother did that with me, I did it with your mother, and she did it with you," my grandmother explained. "It works."

"I don't doubt it," I mumbled while yawning. "But I'm twenty-four years old, and I have no idea of what you're talking about. Can you show me?"

I followed my mother and grandmother as they walked to my bedroom with sure steps. My grandmother picked my little sleep-thief from her crib while my mother crossed her arms, ready to watch what she knew was about to happen. Effortlessly and with the confidence of somebody who's done it more times than she cares to tell, my grandmother flipped Julia forward, head over heels. Then, she gently placed her back in the crib and turned to me, saying, "That's how you restart her internal clock."

To this day, I am in awe at how well this old wives' tale worked, not only with Julia but also with our two other daughters, who would soon join our growing family.

Chapter Three

"I'm pregnant," I said to Alex, whose genuine smile betrayed a bit of panic because Julia was only a little over a year old, and we were still trying to figure out this whole parenting thing with one child—let alone two under the age of two. But we had no time to waste because if the first pregnancy proved anything, it was that nine months could fly by. "We have to move."

"What?" Alex asked, still trying to wrap his head around the fact that he was about to be the father of two children. "Why do we have to move?"

"Because this house is too small for a family of four," I explained as I looked around. I felt overwhelmed by the baby furniture that took over the living room and master bedroom, the piles of baby clothes waiting to be folded spread out on the couch and Julia's room, and the many empty bottles of milk that accumulated in the kitchen sink.

Clearly, we had a whole lot to do before this baby joined the Tronco household.

Alex must've been watching my anxiety levels rise as I looked around the room and immediately said, "Okay, let's start looking for a new house then."

We found a realtor that day and started considering what we wanted in our new home. I knew I wanted to live in a house in the suburbs: lots of room to spread out all their toys, on a safe street where the children could ride their bikes surrounded by friendly neighbors, and so on. We also had a much better budget than when we were first married. Alex's career had truly taken off, and he was working as hard as he could—which also meant that he often went on business trips and worked long nights in the office.

Without even thinking about it twice, we placed our house on the market. But it sold faster than we expected, and we soon found ourselves facing the possibility of having to pay rent while we continued looking for our new home—something that, after doing some math, we found out we couldn't really afford, not if we wanted to buy a house in that kind of neighborhood.

"We'll have to move in with my parents . . . again," I said, as images of the last time Alex and I moved in with my parents flashed before my eyes. After returning from our honeymoon, our first home, which was being built, wasn't ready yet. We tried living in one of my parent's apartments, which was on a main road between two major hospitals and above a Subway sandwich shop. Between the sirens and the smell of the ovens below, we didn't last a week before moving in with my parents for a couple of months.

"But they live in a ranch," Alex said, his tone betraying the dread he must have felt at the mere thought of repeating that experience. "We're going to be so cramped there, especially with all the baby furniture and you being pregnant and all my work stuff and—"

"I know," I interrupted. "Do you have a better solution?"

He didn't, which was why we moved in with my parents for the second time in a handful of years. And it was just as chaotic as Alex thought it would be: we were crammed into a tiny space upstairs with most of our belongings, baby furniture, and boxes full of clothes. But I had little time to think about it because I was so busy with Julia and navigating the home-buying process and my pregnancy. I felt as though I'd blinked, and suddenly, I was nine months pregnant and getting ready to welcome our second baby into the world.

As I was getting closer to my delivery date, however, tragedy struck our family again. My nonna on my father's side passed away. She had suffered from Alzheimer's for a few years and, eventually, succumbed to the terrible disease.

"I did it again," I cried to Alex. "I killed another grandparent with my pregnancy!"

"You know it's not like that," he tried to reassure me—although even he had to admit the timing was eerily coincidental.

Either way, I didn't have much time to ponder it because our second daughter was born soon after, on March 17, after a relatively smooth delivery witnessed by Alex, my mother, mother-in-law, grandmother, sister, sister-in-law, and two aunts. Indeed, the delivery room was just as busy as the first time. We decided to name our daughter Isabella but would call her Bella for short—I wanted to just go with Bella because it means "beautiful" in Italian; however, Alex wanted a more formal name for her, so we settled on Isabella.

Once back home, the reality of having two young children—probably brought on by hormones and restlessness—smacked me right in my face, and I began sobbing. *What have we just done to our family?* Julia used to have our undivided attention, and now we had to somehow split our time between her and our newborn. Bella was also a horrible sleeper, especially at first, and the only way she would fall asleep was if we put her in the car seat and took her for a ride. I guess she found the vibration of the car soothing, but we found this routine, which went on for the first six months of her life, to be exhausting.

While we were thankful that my parents had welcomed us back into their house with two little ones, it didn't take long for their ranch to become way too small for all of us. Although they offered to let us take over their upstairs floor, we were still quite limited on space as a family of four. Alex had virtually no quiet area where he could go and study for the many certifications he was going for—he wanted to get licensed in different types of investments. As a result, he would wait until everyone in the house was asleep and stay up most of the night to focus on his studies, which, of course, took a toll on him in the long run. He had dark circles around his eyes, and his patience routinely ran thin, especially when both children needed our attention.

Fortunately, within a couple of months of living with my parents, we found the house of our dreams: a four-bedroom with about 3,000 square feet. It was in your classic, great basic neighborhood with young families, where it was safe enough for all the children to wait at the bus stop in the morning, and neighbors waved to one another because they all knew each other. One of those neighborhoods where you could just ride your bike without a care in the world, where everyone decorated for Halloween, ready to welcome trick-or-treaters, and you could go and borrow a cup of sugar from the house next door any time you needed it.

But not long after we moved into our new home, I started not feeling too well. I lacked energy, and I felt nauseous. I wanted to attribute it to the move and the fact that the children were so young and needed so much of my attention. But when the symptoms did not subside after a couple of weeks—rather, they intensified—I knew I had to do something I didn't feel ready for: take another pregnancy test.

I bought a few at the local pharmacy and went back home. As I waited for the longest three minutes of my life, I kept thinking how absurd it was that I was even taking a test. It was November 2003, and Bella was born in March of that same year, so there was no way I could have been pregnant. A woman's body doesn't recover that quickly from giving birth, right?

Wrong.

I was pregnant.

Again.

I was about to have three children under three years of age. And now I had to tell Alex.

This time, I decided to show him the pregnancy test instead of announcing the news myself. He looked at me, then at the test, then back at me. Although I knew he felt just as overwhelmed as me, he smiled brightly and hugged me. Then he whispered, "Maybe this time it's a boy!"

Wrong again.

A few weeks later, the doctor confirmed we were expecting our third daughter. "But . . ." I tried to find the right words. "We don't even know what name to give this one!" I heard myself say as if that was reason enough why we couldn't have a third daughter.

The doctor giggled, apparently thinking this was funny. But to me, it was a serious matter. I had no clue what to name her! Still, I thought I would figure it out while waiting for her to be born.

I don't know if it was the fact that having two children was already keeping me so busy or if it was because I still was so involved with decorating the house, but my third pregnancy flew by. And this time, without any deaths in the family (thank goodness).

Suddenly, our third daughter was here, and we still had no name for her. We knew we wanted to keep going with Italian names, and eventually, we settled on Olivia. But let me tell you: Olivia was the worst baby ever! She didn't want to eat; she cried constantly, and she didn't sleep. This time, I was truly on my last resort.

One morning, after our umpteenth sleepless night, I was at my wit's end. I caught Alex before he left for work and said, "I can't do this anymore. You're getting a vasectomy."

Alex didn't protest. He looked at me, nodded, and scheduled a consultation with his doctor a few days later. Not long after that, we put an end to surprise pregnancies.

I thought I was going to be relieved that my days of dealing with non-sleeping, non-eating, and crying newborns were finally over. Instead, I felt a sense of finality, as if a big, important chapter of my life had ended. My emotions swelled, wetting my eyes. *Did we make the right decision?*

At that moment, Julia pulled on my shirt, and my eyes gazed down at her, barely stopping the tears from spilling down my cheeks. She smiled at me and hugged my leg, whispering in her tiny toddler voice, "I love you, Mama." I closed my eyes for a moment and thanked God for the three healthy babies he had gifted me. Yes, this chapter was over, but its most beautiful memories would last a lifetime.

I thanked God for my three healthy babies.

Chapter Four

"My company offered me a promotion!" Alex said the moment he came home from work. He placed his briefcase on the couch, stepped into the kitchen, spun me around, and kissed me.

"Congratulations!" I said and wrapped my arms around him, smiling as I held him tight.

Alex had been working extra hard lately. We had finally moved into our new house and had everything we could have possibly wanted: our daughters had spacious bedrooms, a reading nook, and a toy room—which was originally supposed to be an office, but Alex was always working outside the home, and the kids had so many toys that we needed an extra room to fit them in. Our grand master bedroom had en suite and, no matter how hard my day had been—parenting three daughters so close in age is a gigantic undertaking that I wouldn't recommend to the faint of heart—I always found myself smiling when I walked in. It was truly everything I had ever dreamed of. Lots of fluffy pillows covered our bed, vanilla and lavender-scented candles around the bathtub, and plenty of family photos, including a favorite from our wedding day, decorated the walls. Above our bed hung a wooden cross with Jesus Christ, symbolizing our deep Catholic faith.

Because we love the water so much, we even added an in-ground pool, which might seem odd for Upstate New York, given the weather, but a lot of people have them. Plus, the pool made for a great addition whenever we entertained in our backyard, which was often. Playhouses for the children, bicycles, and what we referred to as "outside toys" dotted the grass around the pool. The rule was if you bring a toy outside and it gets dirty, it's now an outside toy and forbidden from making its way back inside. The girls complained, but it was a way for me to keep most of the dirt outside where it belonged.

But while our home was idyllic, our debt was not. Building a house with all the trimmings from scratch while going from a two-person to a five-person household within a handful of years had done a number on our credit cards, which were charged to the max. I panicked about it constantly. Raising our three daughters had become my full-time job, and even though I still helped at my parents' deli as much as I possibly could, I didn't make nearly as much as I needed to if I wanted to make a real dent in our debt.

Alex, however, would constantly reassure me. "Don't worry, I can always make more money," he'd say. He was paid on commission, and the more clients he helped with their future investments and planning, the more money he made. So, he rolled up his sleeves and, sure enough, he worked his butt off, which was why his promotion was welcomed but not surprising.

"They want me to oversee a whole field," he told me. It was a step up from selling insurance policies. In the new position, he'd manage a whole team of people who sold them in a specific area.

"That's amazing. I'm so proud of you!" I reiterated my congratulations with another kiss and was surprised when Alex took a step back.

Still holding my hands, he said as calmly as he could muster, "There's just one problem. It's in Milwaukee, Wisconsin."

The excitement left me all at once.

No.

We had just settled in our new home, paid off a big chunk of our debt, and our daughters had even found friends to play with in our neighborhood. We couldn't move to Milwaukee. Our support system was right where we were, in Albany, and we'd be completely alone in Wisconsin. What if I needed help with Julia, Bella, or Olivia? Who would I call? I had never lived anywhere but Albany. How could I possibly find a new pediatrician I trusted?

And a move would mean leaving our parents behind, and I wanted them to spend as much time as possible with the kids. Not to mention that I knew my dad relied on me at the deli. I couldn't just abandon them. Our children would be so far away from their grandparents that there would surely be holidays we wouldn't be able to spend together. Just the thought of it was enough to bring tears to my eyes. I loved my grandparents, and the memories I made with them were some of the most precious ones I carried with me. So, moving so far away meant stealing something truly special from all three of my children. Was that the right thing to do?

No.

I wanted to cry and scream. My heart was beating quickly, and I felt my hands tremble as Alex held them. Looking into his eyes, I could tell he was excited about this promotion. And he should have been—it was a big step. He had worked so hard and climbed the corporate ladder quicker than expected: he deserved this. Was I going to stand in the way and prevent him from being proud of his accomplishment?

No.

"Alright, let's do it," I heard myself say.

"Seriously?" Alex smiled tentatively as if wanting to make sure he had heard correctly.

I nodded.

"Yes!" he screamed, picking me up again and spinning around, sealing the deal with a kiss. "I'll call management right now to tell them my answer."

He zoomed out of the kitchen, and I realized that the butter I had been melting in the pan to sauté the green beans had burned. I hated cooking to begin with—and to be completely honest, I wasn't the best at it anyway. Even though I came from a family of proud Italians, and as such, food was always central to our gatherings and family life, cooking for me was a chore. I felt like I lacked the inventiveness one needs in the kitchen, which is probably why my go-to dinner was chicken and green beans or chicken and potatoes on special occasions.

"Darn it," I grumbled, scraping the black and crusted bits off the pan and into the sink. A few tears gathered in my eyes and made their way down my cheeks; I just hoped Alex's call would take long enough for me to get rid of the evidence.

Milwaukee was not on my list of top-ten places to visit, let alone live in. Was the weather going to be even colder than it was in Albany, and would it be possible to get direct flights? And what about the schools? Were they going to be just as good? So many questions crowded my mind. I felt like my lungs wouldn't fill with air.

"Momma." Julia walked into the kitchen, shaking me out of my daze. "I'm hungry."

"Dinner will be ready soon, baby," I said, blinking back some tears as I looked down at her. "Go put your toys away and wash your hands, okay?"

"Okay, Momma," she said, walking back toward her room.

"They're thrilled," Alex said as he snuck up behind me, holding Olivia. "We can put the house on the market tomorrow, and I'll start looking for houses in Milwaukee."

Oh my gosh. It hadn't even occurred to me that we would have to sell our brand-new, beautiful home. All of the work that had gone into making it the house of our dreams, the perfect place to raise our three daughters, one where we could entertain our friends and family . . . would have to be sold. And we would have to move not only to another state and city but also to another neighborhood full of people I had never met. And I didn't want to meet them. I just wanted to stay here with the wonderful neighbors I already had.

"Okay, thank you." It was all I was able to say without letting Alex know how much I was dreading the move.

At dinner, Alex talked nonstop about what this move meant for his career and our family. He acknowledged it would be quite a change but reassured me that the children were young enough to acclimate elsewhere, that we would visit our family often, and we would fly them out to see us as well. It was as if he knew the news had troubled me, even though I had not said anything out loud. His words comforted me, and we began planning our move.

Things evolved faster than I expected, especially because our house went under contract with a potential buyer rather quickly. I hated when the future owners came to see it and take measurements to see if their furniture fit in what was still *our* home. It felt as if they were invading my happy place. When they opened the kitchen cabinets to see how spacious they were, I nearly yelled at them to mind their business. The problem was, it *was* their business to check the cabinets, figure out if their king mattress would fit into the bedroom, and comment on how lovely it was going to be to relax in the en-suite bathroom's candle-lined tub.

When Alex and I told our parents about Milwaukee, their facial expressions revealed they were saddened by it, but their words spoke of support, encouragement, and pride. I shared the news with my close friends, who vowed to visit us as often as they could, making sure we knew they were more than happy to host us should we choose to visit them instead.

As our moving day grew closer, my ability to restrain myself from telling Alex how I really felt grew weaker—until, one day, it completely disappeared. It was the day that I had to take our wedding photo off the wall in our bedroom. I couldn't do it. I suddenly had a flashback to the moment when we chose to hang it there and all of the moments that came before that: stepping into our bedroom for the first time, seeing how big and bright Julia's eyes got when she saw the toy room, our back-and-forth with the contractors on which tiles to use where, what color to paint the walls, and everything that had gone into turning this idea of a house into a home. *Our* home. I couldn't take that photo off the wall because it would make the move all too real. So, I turned to Alex, who was standing there looking at me, sighed, and said, "I can't do this."

"I know," Alex said. "I have seen you struggle with the move and felt this moment would come. And I am here to tell you that it's okay."

"But we are under contract," I said, feeling both torn and relieved.

"We can get out." He walked closer to me. "It'll cost us, but we still have time. I don't want to move if it's going to make you miserable. If you're miserable, I am too, and so are our daughters. And our family doesn't need to go through that. I want us to be happy."

"But your job, your promotion . . ." I said, feeling as though my heart was going to beat out of my chest.

"I'm a great salesman," he said, smiling at me. "I can go back to selling life insurance. If the company values me enough to offer this promotion, they will offer me another one here in Albany when the opportunity arises."

I couldn't believe his words—actually, I could. I knew exactly the kind of man I had married. He was perfect in every sense of the word. Never one to shy away from showing me how much he loved me, he once sent me flowers to Julia's preschool because he knew I was volunteering there on Mother's Day. An "Aww" erupted from the other women when they saw the florist present me with this beautiful bouquet. Alex was just as attentive with our daughters. He was an adoring father who would say things like, "Let's go for a bike ride!" when he was home from work and the weather allowed it, or, "Time to put up the Christmas lights!" when it was that time of year, or, "Girls, let's go build a snowman!" after it had snowed enough.

He was so thoughtful, kind, and loving that my girl-friends teased me when we got together for Bunco nights. Every other week, we would designate someone to be our host, and we'd each bring something to eat or drink. Then, as we played, my girlfriends would talk trash about their husbands, adding, "Don't worry, Gina. You don't have to contribute to this conversation; we know Alex is perfect." To which I would reply with a smile and a nod every time.

I knew exactly the kind of man I had married.

Alex was the kind of husband who always invited me on his business trips, and although I would have loved to go on each and every one of them, I knew that I couldn't always leave Julia, Bella, and Olivia with my mom or mother-in-law. So, I would accompany him to major events, where he always made me feel like the center of attention by introducing me to everybody in the room, speaking highly of how lucky he was to be my husband. He always made me feel cherished and would often organize weekend getaways for just the two of us, somewhere close, like Vermont, that we could get to by car.

But each trip, no matter how short-lived because of the demands of work and parenthood always called, was like the Fourth of July. And once again, Alex was now showing me just how much he loved me and cared about my feelings by walking away from a huge promotion just to make me happy.

That night, when I went to bed, I looked at our wedding photo on the wall and smiled. I really had the most perfect husband in the world.

Chapter Five

"Hi, Mom!" Julia, Bella, and Olivia greeted me in unison when they entered the car. They had the biggest, brightest smile on their faces.

"Ready to go pack?" I asked as I shifted the car from park to drive and left their school to head home.

"YES!" they all said, clapping their hands.

Over the years, it had become a family tradition to go to Disney World in Florida during spring break, and this year was no exception. I glanced back at them through the rearview mirror and felt a tingling sensation in my heart when I saw how much their eyes sparkled with joy and anticipation. *Enjoy it while it lasts, Gina*, I told myself. I know it's a cliché, but I just couldn't believe how quickly they grew up.

Enjoy it while it lasts, Gina, I told myself.

Julia was twelve years old, Bella was ten, and Olivia was nine. One moment I was trying to juggle feeding schedules and diaper changes, and the next, I was dealing with questions from Julia: "Why can't I put lipstick on yet? All the other girls at school wear it!" and Bella, "Mooooom, Olivia took my favorite T-shirt again, and now I have nothing to wear!" and Olivia, "Mom, I need my privacy when I talk on the phone with my friends," which was usually followed by a *SLAM!* as she shut the bedroom door behind her back.

Yes, my daughters were growing up fast. And while I couldn't wait for them to grow up when they were infants and toddlers—having to run after two toddlers who had recently learned how to walk was no easy feat—now, I sure missed those days. But they reminded me how important it was to appreciate the time we had together because it goes by too fast.

So there I was, smiling as I drove the four of us back home. It was mid-February, and the roads were not too bad: Albany had recently had yet another snowstorm that painted the entire town white. It made for a rather picturesque landscape, especially the tall pine trees with the accumulated snow on the branches. But the thirty-degree weather only made us dream of sunny Florida even more.

"Is Dad home yet?" Julia asked.

"No, he can't get out of work early today," I said as I drove slower than usual to make sure I didn't hit any black ice on accident—the thin coating of ice on the dark paved street could be dangerous, and I certainly didn't want to risk anything.

"It's too bad, though, that we can get out of school early when we go to Disney, but he can't," Olivia complained.

"I know, Liv, his job is demanding," I said, squinting my eyes because the sun suddenly hit the icy road, blinding me. "But we'll have him all for us for ten days!"

"Whoo-hoo!" Bella said.

A few minutes later, we arrived home, and the girls began packing right away.

"Don't forget to wear the clothes you want to travel in before you go to bed tonight," I reminded them. This was something we also did every year so that we wouldn't waste any time getting dressed in the morning.

Fortunately for us, there was a direct flight from Albany to Orlando. Once there, we would hop on the Magic Express Bus—Disney's shuttle from the airport to its many resorts. This year, however, I decided that it might be best to rent a car at the Orlando airport and drive to Disney's Beach Club Resort ourselves. We didn't want to have to wait for the bus to stop at all the other resorts before reaching our destination; now that the girls were older, we wanted to hit the ground running right away.

The afternoon went by quickly. By the time Alex came home from work, the girls were about to go to bed.

"See you in the morning!" Alex said, his tone filled with joy and anticipation with what we all knew was going to be yet another magical family vacation.

Just like every year, the girls woke up before the alarm clock went off—funny how they could wake up early every day of our family vacation but not when it was time to go to school. Already dressed, they put their Minnie ears on, and off we went to the airport, where, given the early morning flight—it left around six o'clock—there were very few people around, which meant the lines went by fast.

Given that the flight would take about three hours, we often tried to get a few more hours of sleep while waiting to arrive at our destination. But the adrenaline rushing through our veins always made it difficult for us to calm down and rest. The part I loved the most about our flight to Orlando was the landing: the moment we were low enough to the ground to spot the first palm trees always made my heart smile, and the girls would shout, "We're here!"

Warm sunshine greeted us the moment we got off the airplane, prompting us to take off our sweatshirts and instantly making us forget about the icy roads back in New York. At the baggage claim, the girls always raced each other to see who spotted the luggage first. Over the years, our pieces of luggage had increased dramatically, going from two smaller ones to at least four big ones because of all the clothes the girls wanted to bring with them, which included all the just-in-cases: elegant dresses, running shoes, and just-in-case-it-rains clothing options.

"The car should be ready," I said as we made our way toward the rental counters. The airport was not as crowded as I imagined it was during the summertime when most people had time off work and, therefore, time for a vacation. We thought of going to Disney twice a year—spring break and summertime—but with how hot it is in Florida during the summer months, we opted for just February break.

Not to mention, we always had a busy summer with all the sports tournaments the girls had: soccer, tennis, and dance. They had recently stopped taking piano lessons—they shared the same love for music that I had and had learned to play piano very well over the years. But what I thought would be a free hour or so in my afternoons was filled out quickly with yet another sport activity. Don't get me wrong, I was happy the girls had so many interests, and they really applied themselves to everything they did. But our late afternoons, weekends, and summers were always filled with a hectic schedule that allowed for no relaxation time.

Alex and I would often have to split because, even though the girls were close in age and attending the same sport matches or events, they were in different groups and teams, which meant that they would often be in separate hotels or even cities. And since I was only one person and had yet to figure out how to be in two cities or hotels at the same time, Alex would have to help out, which he never hesitated to do anyhow. I think this is also why these family vacations were so special, not only to our daughters but also to us.

As years went by, the girls developed such a demanding schedule between school and sports activities that Alex and I began spending less time with each other since we were so busy parenting. Like two ships passing each other in port, Alex and I often left the house at the same time on weekends but drove to two completely different places. I could be going to Boston and Alex to Philadelphia, for example, to attend two different soccer matches at different times of the day, only to meet each other at the end of the weekend once back home, usually late at night, exhausted and dreading the work week and the same old routine to begin again the very next day.

Alex and I were like two ships passing each other in port.

But finally, we were on vacation.

"The Beach Club!" the girls shouted in unison when they saw the entrance from the back seat of our rental car.

"We're home!" Alex said as he slowed down to look for a parking spot.

The Beach Club Resort was our hotel of choice at Disney World. It had that beachy vibe we craved—especially coming from cold New York—with a gorgeous pool, a well-equipped gym, and a great selection of places to eat. Plus, it was within walking distance of Epcot and Hollywood Studios, two of our favorite Disney theme parks. Oh, who am I kidding? We loved every single park, no exceptions.

"Are you thinking what I'm thinking?" Julia asked Bella and Olivia.

"One moment, girls," I said, getting the feeling I knew what she was referring to.

We had just entered our room, which was a spacious one-bedroom suite with a small kitchen equipped with a coffee maker, stove, and oven, as well as a microwave, sink, and a small fridge in case we wanted to cook for ourselves. This was obviously a big, fat *no* because I was on vacation, and there was absolutely no way I was going to cook. The living room had a cream-colored couch that doubled as a queen bed and a light blue armchair, which turned into a twin bed.

Our master bedroom had a king bed and en-suite bathroom, which we didn't have to share with our girls because there was another bathroom in the main room. The white balcony had two blue chairs with a small coffee table between them and offered us a beautiful view of the pool area. The bedroom décor was all about the beach, with photos of sea-shells, waves, and sand—as well as paintings of Minnie and Mickey Mouse on the beach, watching the waves crash ashore.

"EPCOT!" the girls yelled, shaking me out of my daze.

Yep, that's what I thought.

It was almost eleven o'clock in the morning, and even though we had just arrived, the girls couldn't wait to go to the park. So, after a quick bathroom break, we walked over to Epcot to mark yet another family tradition: lunch at La Hacienda de San Angel restaurant in the Mexico pavilion.

Epcot—which stands for Experimental Prototype Community of Tomorrow—is one of the five Disney World parks. Legend has it that Walt Disney was so frustrated with city life—he hated being woken up early by the noise of the garbage truck, among many other things—that he wanted to create the city of the future, circular in shape with a hub in the center for people to gather, homes and businesses all around it, and a railroad. While his utopian city didn't quite pan out, what eventually became of Epcot was something far more enjoyable, in my opinion, for visitors. With a geodesic sphere at the entrance, which hosts one of my favorite rides (Spaceship Earth), Epcot is home to the famous world showcase, with its eleven pavilions, each representing a different country: from Canada, England, France, Japan, and Italy, to the USA, Morocco, Germany, Norway, China, and Mexico.

Walking through the world showcase, visiting all the stores with their original and authentic souvenirs, and eating the different cuisine in every country are some of my most favorite activities. The walk is shorter than it might look, at a little over one and a half miles, but it is exciting how each pavilion has its own flare, smells—the spice rack in Morocco is divine!—and sounds (the mandolin strumming tunes in Italy make you feel like you've been transported to the actual country, especially when it's paired to the just-baked, mouthwatering smell of pizza).

"The three caballeros!" Olivia shouted when we saw the Mayan pyramid, which characterizes the Mexican pavilion in Epcot.

"Alright, let's go," Alex said, walking ahead and leading the group. I could tell he was even more excited than the girls. He cherished these family traditions as much as I did, if not more, because he, too, knew that soon our girls would become adults and perhaps no longer want to come on family vacations with us. So, we both tried to soak up as much as possible of these precious moments. And one of them was going on the Three Caballeros ride inside the Mayan pyramid before having lunch at the La Hacienda restaurant in front of it.

La Hacienda never disappointed. The bottomless chips and salsa, fun and refreshing fruity drinks, along with the cheesy and fragrant meals were exactly what kept us going back every time we went there.

"Girls, so when we go back ho—" I started to say but was interrupted by a single, straightforward . . .

"NO!" the girls said in unison.

"We don't talk about going back to you-know-where on vacation, remember?" Alex reprimanded me.

True. I forgot. One of our rules was that during our ten-day vacation, we could not speak, reference, or even *think* about going back home. That topic was off the table. Taboo. Forbidden. All that was allowed to exist during these fun days was just that: fun at Disney.

I mouthed, "Sorry," and went back for more chips and salsa and another fresh and zesty margarita. Life was good.

Life was good. So good, in fact, that the ten days flew by. As usual, the girls spent the departure day sobbing, vowing to be back soon, and thinking back on all the fun experiences we had.

"Remember when Dad got *soaking wet* on Splash Mountain?" Julia said, laughing and crying at the same time as she recalled the sight of her dad totally soaked when he exited the rollercoaster.

Alex laughed, too, as he hugged her. The two of them, along with Bella, were three peas in a pod. Every day of our vacation, Alex and I woke up before the girls did and went to the gym to work out together. Then, we went back to our room and woke up the girls, who got dressed while we took a shower and got ready for the day.

After breakfast at the resort, we would go to the park and arrive there before it opened—usually at around eight in the morning—and waited for the rope to drop at nine o'clock. Alex was always the first to sprint into action and run all the way to the most popular rides so that he could be, along with Julia and Bella, one of the first—if not *the* first—people in line. Olivia and I, instead, were not big rollercoaster fans, so we either waited for them to be done tasting their breakfast all over again as it came back up while doing a loop de loop, or we would go on calmer rides.

"I think this was the first time we got *real* princess dresses at the Bibbidi Bobbidi Boutique, wasn't it?" Bella asked.

"Yep, first time," I said, smiling. Every year, the girls would get their princess hair makeover at the Bibbidi Bobbidi Boutique—named after Cinderella's fairy godmother's magic spell. Their hair would be pulled so tight and styled in a tall bun with glitter all over it.

Although it must have been uncomfortable, the girls never complained that their heads hurt; God bless them. And while their hair looked beautiful—especially because they would also add a small crown to mark the princess makeover—it was so expensive that, before this year, we could barely afford it.

The Bibbidi Bobbidi Boutique also offered the complete princess makeover, which also included real Disney princess dresses, but they were way too expensive for us at first. So, in an attempt to not make our daughters feel like they didn't really get a real princess treatment, we bought princess dresses at Marshall's as opposed to the parks, where they would cost three times as much—and yes, looked way better and of much better quality than what we could afford.

This year, however, we decided to save up specifically for the all-inclusive Bibbidi Bobbidi Boutique experience, which also consisted of a manicure. The girls got to choose which princess they wanted to be and chose Cinderella, Rapunzel, and Snow White. Julia, who chose

Cinderella, felt a bit more self-conscious than her sisters because, at twelve years old, she was already turning into a young woman. And while she would never, ever, under any circumstance, mention this makeover to her friends back home, the beauty of Disney magic is that no matter your age, you always feel childlike.

And I was glad to see Julia embrace this occasion and choose to have a princess makeover like she and her sisters did every year. Also, because I believe this was going to be the last time she was able to get one, given the age restrictions in place at the boutique—if they allowed every age group to get one, I am pretty sure I would have gotten one myself every year, too, while Alex would have certainly gone for the pirate makeover they also offered to boys.

"Ladies and gentlemen, it is now time to board the flight," we heard the flight attendant announce that our flight was ready for boarding. We looked at one another and shrugged with a heavy sigh.

"See you real soon, Disney," Olivia said as she glanced back at the Orlando airport one more time before boarding the flight.

Alex hugged her and kissed her forehead before walking on the plane with her while I was the last one of the family to join them. And all I could think of was how lucky I was to have found such a wonderful family man who gave me three beautiful, intelligent, and kind daughters.

I felt so lucky to have found such a wonderful family man.

The flight attendant closed the door to the airplane and began demonstrating safety procedures. It was time to go home, to our regularly scheduled program, to our carpools and sports tournaments. But with another magical Tronco family vacation in the books.

Chapter Six

"*Please wait for our next available agent,*" the pre-recorded voice said for what seemed the umpteenth time.

Drumming my fingers on the kitchen table, I released a deep sigh as I waited for someone to finally answer my call so I could make that reservation for two at Nobu restaurant in Malibu. I glanced at the wall clock in the kitchen: three o'clock. That meant I had been on hold for two hours!

"*Your call is important to us,*" the voice said.

And the call was important to me, too, because I had promised Julia that I would make it happen. She was going to graduate eighth grade in three months, and Alex and I had decided to start a new family tradition: he would take each of our girls on a father-daughter trip when they graduated eighth grade, and I would take them on a mother-daughter trip when they graduated high school. The destination would be up to them, and Julia had chosen Los Angeles, much to the jealousy of Bella and Olivia, who couldn't wait to go to the City of Angels as well.

"What if I see Kim Kardashian?" Julia said, jumping up and down as she daydreamed of meeting her idol. "I have got to go to where the Kardashians usually hang out. Nobu!"

It was 2014, and in the Tronco household, "Keeping Up with the Kardashians" was a regular fixture. Julia, Bella, and Olivia were obsessed with the famous sisters. I didn't get the excitement or why these young women were famous, but I learned that asking what made them famous or why they mattered so much would always bring the same answer from my daughters: "Mommm, you're old! You just don't get it!"

It was true. I didn't get it. Still, there I was, waiting on hold for hours in the hope of making a dinner reservation for Alex and Julia three months in advance.

When I asked Julia why it had to be this specific restaurant, she explained, "Because the Kardashians are always there, shooting their TV show, and it's one of the best places to spot them if you're in LA. They just celebrated a birthday at Nobu, and it's like the coolest restaurant in town because of the Kardashians! You can't go to LA and not eat at Nobu, Mom." She rolled her eyes at me. And I couldn't get over the fact that the little girl who used to style her hair in pigtails and tell just about anyone who would listen that "My mama knows everything" was now a teenager, her hair long and straight, reminding me of just how much I didn't know.

My girl was growing up fast and about to start high school. That thought made me feel proud and scared all at the same time. Proud because of the young woman Julia was becoming, a confident athlete with strong family values and good grades; scared because she was at that age where children begin to push their boundaries as they evolve into their own people and relate more to their peers than their parents.

"Hello, this is Sheila. Thank you for calling Nobu. How may I help you?" the hostess said all in one breath.

"Uhm, yes, hello." I had been on hold for so long that it took me a minute to remember what I was calling for. "I'd like to make a reservation for two, please."

As hard as it was to get a hold of the restaurant, I was happily surprised at how easy it was to reserve a table at the hottest place in Los Angeles.

"Mom, you're the best!" Julia said after I gave her the news later that day when I picked her up from school. Her bright eyes and big smile made me feel like I had just scored a huge win.

Over the years, I had learned to take my parenting wins where I found them: getting rid of a spider in the girls' bathroom even though I was more terrified of it than them resulted in a hug and my daughters crediting me with "saving their lives"; ordering out for the fourth night in a row after my attempt at making dinner went nowhere—but the trash can—turned me into a legend among their friends because "their moms never let them eat take out"; and letting them stay up late to finish watching a show so I could hopefully sleep in the next morning earned me the title of Coolest Mom in the Whole World. So, trading two hours of my life to make a reservation at what was apparently the hardest Japanese restaurant in LA to get into, just to hear my firstborn say I was the best, was worth it.

Fueled by my momentum, I decided to go the extra mile and get her a room at the Beverly Hills Hotel, the ultimate glamourous destination where all the A-list Hollywood stars stayed—which I hoped would include people like the

Kardashians. I didn't think Julia would be impressed if I mentioned Elizabeth Taylor. The Hollywood gods were on my side because I was successful yet again: a deluxe room with a balcony booked for four nights. When I told Julia, she hugged me and said, "Oh Em Gee, I have to go call my friends and tell them!" I knew if she had the urge to call her friends right away, I must have really done well, which made me feel better about the prospect of telling Alex that the room was over $1,000 a night.

"Anything for my girls," Alex said when I told him. He had just come home from work, and even though he was tired, he still managed to smile at me and kiss me on the cheek to reassure me about my decision.

"So the price doesn't bother you?" I asked, my questioning tone conveying I was afraid I had gone too far this time.

"Why would it?" Alex said, shrugging. "That's why we work hard: to give our daughters everything they deserve. Plus, Julia has applied herself in school so far, she is such a sweet and sensitive girl, and she is also committed to her after-school activities. She's got a good head on her shoulders, just like her mama." He winked.

"I agree," I said, smiling at him.

"You know," Alex said in a low tone to make sure the girls wouldn't hear him, even though they were already in bed. "I was also thinking I should rent a sports car, like a convertible, so we can cruise around in style. What do you think?"

"She is going to LOVE it!" I said. I was so excited for Julia that I was kind of regretting that it was going to be just the two of them, as opposed to the whole family—this mini vacation was turning out to be amazing. "But I think we should set some boundaries, you know?"

"Like what?" Alex asked.

"Well, I want Julia to have a good time, but I also want her to keep in mind that this trip is a gift for her eighth-grade graduation, and I want to make sure she stays in that headspace of 'school is important.'"

"Good point," Alex said, taking a seat at the dinner table as I placed a warmed-up plate of Chinese food in front of him. "What do you have in mind?"

"What if we tell her that she has to go tour a college campus?" I said, sitting next to him and joining him for dinner.

"Great idea!" Alex said, digging into his Kung Pao chicken. "What about Pepperdine or UCLA?"

"Sounds good to me," I said, enjoying my egg-fried rice. "We'll make sure that each girl, on their eighth-grade graduation trip, gets to visit a college campus."

And we toasted to that.

As the months turned into weeks and the weeks dissolved into days, Julia was getting more and more excited about her upcoming trip. She asked if she could spend a day at the beach in Malibu, which Alex and I agreed to. Before we knew it, it was time for them to leave for Los Angeles.

The morning they left, I walked them to Alex's car, which they would leave at the airport in the long-term parking lot. I hugged and kissed them both before reminding them to keep updated on how their trip was going.

Two hours later, my phone rang.

"Hey, Mom," Julia said on the phone. "We just landed at JFK, and now we have an hour to make the connection."

"Alright, honey," I said, smiling, even though she couldn't see me. "How was the flight to New York City?"

"Good," she said. "Dad slept, but I couldn't because I'm too excited!"

"Well, you know your dad can fall asleep at the drop of a dime." I giggled. "Just let me know when you guys are on the other flight to Los Angeles, okay?"

"Okay, Mom," Julia said. "Here's Dad. He wants to say hi."

"Hi, honey," Alex greeted me. "How are my girls doing?"

"Aww, we're good," I said, feeling my cheeks turning red. Alex was always so sweet . . . I couldn't believe that, after so many years of marriage and three daughters who—God love them—tested our patience and limits every single day, he could still make me feel butterflies in my stomach as if we were teenagers on our first date. "We miss you already."

"We miss you, too, honey," he said, his voice getting a bit lost among all the commotion of the airport in the background.

"Oh, I wanted to tell you that Lori texted me and asked if the girls and I would be up for a trip to Wildwood," I told him. Lori was a dear family friend whose youngest daughter was the same age as Julia. I met her many years prior, given she was a valued customer at my parents' store.

"Oh, that's a great idea!" Alex said. "This way, you guys won't be alone waiting for us to come back."

"Exactly," I said. "I told her a few days ago that you and Julia would be leaving for Los Angeles, and she also invited some other friends from soccer practice so we can all be together and have fun at the beach. We'll be staying at a local hotel."

"Awesome," Alex said. "Glad to hear that. Hey, hun, we need to pick up our pace and get to the other gate. It's a ways away, so we'll call you when we are on the plane, okay?"

"Sounds good," I said. "Be safe and look after Julia."

"I know, don't worry," he said, sighing because I always told him to look after whichever daughter he had with him as if they were all still babies. What can I say? In a mother's heart, children never grow up. "Give Bella and Liv a kiss from me."

Once the call ended, I went to Bella and Olivia's bedroom to help them pack for the four-night stay in New Jersey. I shouldn't have been surprised when I saw they were ready to go—both of them even had a bikini on underneath their jeans and T-shirt. I had already gotten my bag packed, so all that was left to do was take our things to the car and drive to Wildwood.

We arrived five hours later, and the girls went straight to the beach while I checked in to the hotel.

"Room 218," said the lady at the front desk as she handed me the electronic room key.

"Thank you," I said and made my way to the room.

I walked out of the elevator and smelled the stale stench of cigarette smoke. Given the many No Smoking signs plastered everywhere throughout the hotel, I could only assume that the stench was due to the carpets that had not been replaced since the Smokefree Air Act law, which prohibited smoking in public places, went into effect in New Jersey in 2006.

"Great," I said, as I held my breath in as much as possible while walking to my room.

I opened the door and was less than impressed by what I saw: the queen-sized beds were covered by faded blankets that had clearly undergone years and years of heavy washing with industrial solvents. The sheets were stained with bleach, and the pillows were harder than rocks. I sighed and walked to the bathroom. The toilet seat was chipped, and the water pressure in the shower was quite low.

"Must be from all the calcium buildup on this showerhead," I said to no one.

This was definitely not the same hotel room that Alex and Julia would soon be enjoying. But this was certainly a typical accommodation for Wildwood, just nothing to write home about.

After I was done taking our clothes out of our bags, I checked the time and realized that Alex and Julia still had about two more hours before they got to LA—the direct flight from JFK to LAX took about six hours. So, I decided to go downstairs and join Bella and Olivia at the beach.

"Mom," Olivia said, "Bella and I decided that when we graduate eighth grade, we also want to go to Los Angeles with Dad."

"Sounds good to me," I said, smiling because I'd anticipated them wanting to have the same experience as their older sister—I knew they wouldn't want to feel like they missed out on something so special. "What about when you graduate high school and go on a trip with me?"

"That's too far in the future, Mom," Bella admonished me. "Nobody thinks that far out."

Ugh, to be young and carefree, I thought to myself.

Our other friends arrived soon after us, and their children, who were more or less around my girls' age, ran to the beach to have fun with Bella and Olivia. We all knew each other from soccer practice and had become good friends over the years.

We sipped coffee while watching our children have fun. Then my phone rang.

"We just landed!" read the text I received from Julia. "We'll call when we get off the plane. OMG, I'm in LA!"

I could tell she was excited and felt so grateful that Alex had taken time off of work to take her on the trip of a lifetime.

The photos that Julia and Alex sent me on their mini vacation only confirmed just how much fun they were having: Julia with her arms up in the air, a bright smile, and the Hollywood sign in the background; Julia's hair flowing in the wind as they cruised around Malibu in the rented convertible; Alex carrying all of Julia's bags while she shopped in Rodeo Drive; pictures of the delicious food they ate at Nobu; and Julia's sad expression when she realized that their celebrity homes tour wouldn't go as planned since tall trees protected the houses and, therefore, were not visible from the outside.

Time flew by for them and for us, as we also kept busy at the beach and had fun with our friends. We left New Jersey the same day Alex and Julia flew back home, and we met them at the house with open arms.

"I brought you a gift from Rodeo Drive," Alex said, kissing me on the cheek. He took a rectangular-shaped box out of the carry-on luggage and handed it to me. But even before I opened it, I felt my heart beating a bit faster than usual because the box was of a light blueish green, almost teal, with the words "TIFFANY & CO." written on it in black letters. My jaw dropped the moment I saw the gorgeous bracelet.

"Do you like it?" he asked.

"I love it," I whispered. "Thank you so much!"

Alex helped me put it on, and I couldn't stop looking at it.

Meanwhile, we could hear Julia, who was in the living room, telling her sisters everything she saw and giving them tips on what to see and do when they graduated eighth grade and went on the same trip.

"You have got to go to Rodeo Drive," she said. "That's where Dad got me my Louis Vuitton bag. You'll have such a good time there, trust me. But I think that for my next trip, I want to get out of the country and be even more adventurous."

"What do you mean?" Bella asked.

"I was thinking about going to Mexico," Julia said.

"That sounds like fun!" Olivia added.

Alex and I looked at each other and shrugged.

"Well, I guess we better start saving for her Sweet 16, huh?" Alex said, and we both laughed.

PART TWO
My World Fell Apart

Chapter Seven

I had the perfect life: a loving husband, healthy and happy daughters, and the dream house. My entire adult life was dedicated to my family, making sure to raise my daughters with good values so they would succeed in the world and be kind human beings.

Every day I thanked God for giving me such a wonderful partner, a real family man, who always put our needs above his and made sure that none of his "four girls," as he called us, felt unappreciated or left out or taken for granted.

Every day I thanked God for giving me such a wonderful partner who always put our needs above his.

And then, life changed.

Forever.

Within a few seconds.

†

It was July 3, 2017. 8:58 a.m. when I found out Alex was having an affair. We had been in Mexico for less than twenty-four hours, and my heart was beating so hard in my chest that I could actually hear it. The sound was deafening, the pounding so hard it hurt. It felt as if my chest would explode at any moment. I couldn't breathe. But if I gasped for air, that would have grounded me enough to make the moment all too real.

Alex is having an affair.

The words echoed louder and louder inside my head.

"I'm going to get the girls from breakfast," Alex said. "They're going to worry if they don't see at least one of us there."

He glanced at me but quickly looked down to the floor as if not wishing to meet my eyes. Then he closed the door behind him.

I placed my trembling hand over my chest as if to try to calm it down. Instead, I felt the pain radiate, and my lips parted, drying up and quickly cracking.

My body was shivering. No oxygen. My fingers, still holding onto the phone, were trembling.

I'm falling.

Was I falling? My head was spinning, but the floor was steady beneath my feet.

It's cold.

I looked down and realized I didn't have my flip-flops on. I was barefoot.

As I raised my eyes, they met the phone that was still in my hand.

The photo, his photo, her photo, was staring back at me even though Alex had deleted it—it was imprinted on my mind. It was mocking me, reveling in the destruction it had caused as my life imploded with the force of a nuclear bomb.

Air.

My limbs felt weaker and weaker.

Suddenly, I saw Alex and me at the Super Dance in high school, sitting close to one another, talking as I shyly tucked my long, brown hair behind my ear. I blinked, and I was at my parents' house, where I found the path of rose petals through the hall leading up to their kitchen, me tip-toeing my way through the flowers until I saw Alex on one knee, looking up at me with trembling hands, asking me to marry him. I looked away and saw him picking me up and walking me through the threshold of our first house after we came back home from our honeymoon. I was smiling and giggling.

A flash brought me to the hospital room, where I saw Alex holding baby Julia for the first time, his eyes wet with joyful tears as he kept whispering, *"I'm a daddy!"* His voice guided me to the moment he opened the door of our dream home for the first time after coming back from work and greeted the four of us with, *"Girls, I'm home!"* I saw our family trips to Disney, Alex in the front row waiting for the character parade as he danced along to the music, his arms raised high as we went on rollercoasters with our daughters, his lips on mine when he kissed me with the princess castle in the background beautifully framed by the colorful fireworks.

I blinked again and saw him driving our daughters to soccer practice, helping them with their homework, bringing me flowers just because, calling me from work to see how my day was going, staying up all night when the girls were sick, taking me on business trips with him, introducing me to everyone and anyone around as his better half, sitting next to me on the airplane to Mexico, working out with me that morning at the gym, and . . . and . . .

I was gasping for air.

As the oxygen traveled through me, I felt a tingling sensation rushing down my arms, hands, and legs as if millions of invisible needles were poking me over and over again. I looked around and saw my reflection in the tall mirror: I was still standing in front of the nightstand, still wearing my workout clothes stained with sweat, and still holding my phone.

My breathing was labored but consistent.

I dropped the phone quickly as if I had just realized I had been holding a boiling pot of water with no oven mitts on.

Where is he? He had been gone to see the girls for what felt like an eternity.

It could have been a few seconds, but that didn't even matter. I didn't want to talk to him. I didn't want to see him. I didn't want to be with him.

I rushed to the bathroom and crawled on top of the wooden bath caddy—much larger and steadier than any I had seen before. As I curled into the fetal position, my heart and lungs exploded in excruciating pain of tears and sobs.

Alex is having an affair.

What was to become of my life? What was to become of my family? What was to become of my life? What was to become of my family?

My parents had taught me many things when I was growing up: how to ride a bike, how to tie my shoes, how to take an order at the deli, how to make my bed, how to be polite. Through them, I learned the importance of respecting my elders, making sure that family always came first, and that hard work was the only gateway to success and fulfillment. But they had never taught me what to do if my husband cheated on me, if my life shattered within seconds, or if my family fell apart.

I hugged my knees, bringing them closer to my chin.

None of this made sense. Maybe this wasn't happening. Maybe this was a nightmare, and I was about to wake up. I squeezed my eyes, willing the tears to stop rushing down my cheeks. Could I forgive him? It was up to me—and if I forgave him, maybe things could go back to normal.

But the memory of that photo had seared itself across my vision, and I quickly closed my eyes again.

It's true.

Alex had an affair; Alex cheated on me; Alex destroyed our family forever. If I forgave him, I would teach my girls that it is OK to be disrespected by a man and take him back. I couldn't do that. But I wanted to. I didn't want to be a mother at that moment, just a hurt woman. Could I just be me, Gina?

Oh my God, the girls. They were going to be devastated when they found out. Because I was going to tell them. I was going to yell it from the rooftop at anybody who would listen that Alex had cheated on me. I was going to ruin his reputation, rat him out at work, and make his life a living nightmare like he had made mine. He deserved what was coming to him. I would take him for all he was worth, leave him with not even a cent to his name. He would have to answer to our family, the court, and God. I was going to ensure he felt even more pain than I was feeling at that moment.

Alex would have to answer to our family, the court, and God.

But I couldn't do that to him—to the girls, to me, to us. He was a good guy who had made a bad, bad mistake. But didn't that make him evil? Of course it didn't. Could I find it in my heart to forgive him? I wasn't sure. Or we would just go to couples' therapy, he would repent, fix what he had broken, and we would be back to planning the next Tronco family trip in no time. He would still come home to us every evening after work. We would still be Gina and Alex, the couple all of our friends envied because of the perfect marriage we had.

I love him.

No! I hated him with every fiber of my being. He had broken me in a way I didn't think was humanly possible. How was I ever going to recover from this? I couldn't see an end in sight. No light. No hope. Would I have to spend the rest of my life pretending this never happened? That he never cheated on me? That I never saw that photo?

The photo.

I squeezed my eyes.

I hate him.

No—I couldn't hate him. He had gifted me with the best years of my life. We were high school sweethearts. We were each other's first love. We had three daughters. He'd held my hand while I was in labor, kissed my forehead when I had the flu. Alex told me how beautiful I was every chance he got. He didn't need to have an affair; I had already given him everything.

Sure, our life as Mom and Dad was hectic and full of errands that had to be run, events that had to be attended, and bills that had to be paid. Yes, we sometimes struggled to stay awake while watching a movie together on a Friday night because we were so exhausted from a week that had been full of things to do. And yes, we had to make a real effort to dress up and go out to dinner, just the two of us, even though ordering takeout and chilling in our pajamas felt much easier, but we did it anyway—having children can truly push your marriage to the back burner, so making time for one another was something we felt we needed to do to keep our marriage healthy.

We remembered every important day. We celebrated every special occasion and never kept anything from one another, regardless of how bad it was.

Except the affair.

Except the affair. This was just a bump on the road, though—a big one that had caused damage. But was the damage irreparable? What decision would most honor God?

I opened my eyes and slowly got off the bath caddy. I walked to the sink and washed my face with tepid water. The sensation of the lukewarm drops slowly caressing my skin, scarred with bitter tears, felt like healing from a bad burn. I felt my skin breathe in, my lips taste life, and my eyes welcome light.

I had made a decision, and I knew it.

I looked at my reflection in the mirror and whispered, "We have to get through this."

Chapter Eight

"We were together for two months," Alex said. "It meant absolutely nothing, I promise."

He was sitting in the chair by the desk. I was sitting on the bed with my back propped up against the headboard, my arms crossed and close to my chest. I was staring at him, my mouth tense. Although he was directly facing me, he didn't dare to look me in the eyes.

"I am so sorry," he said. "I will fix this, I promise. I made a terrible mistake, and I swear I am going to do all I can and more to fix this, fix *us*."

I could tell Alex was emotional because I heard in his trembling voice that he was working hard to hold back tears.

A bright ray of sun peeked through the slightly open blinds of our resort room and hit me right in the face, making me squint. I readjusted myself on the bed but still had to shield my eyes against the bright light with one hand. My chest was no longer protected by my crossed arms, which made me feel even more vulnerable to what was going on.

"I met her at the bank," Alex said.

I wanted to punch him in the face.

Then, Alex went on to add details about who she was, details I refused to listen to. I would not allow him to add color to my nightmares. To me, she did not have a name, even though he volunteered one. To me, she did not have a profession, even though he specified it. To me, she was just a sleazy homewrecker. And Alex was the idiot who had fallen for her games.

"Why?" I managed to voice the one coherent question floating around in my turbulent mind. My tone was thin but determined, the one word hitting him straight in the heart. I deserved to know why he had cheated on me. What did she give him that I hadn't in almost three decades? I had given him a family, a sense of stability, a routine. What did she have that I didn't? I worked out regularly and ate a clean diet, so I knew I looked pretty darn good for a mother to three daughters. So, why did he cheat?

Silence.

Alex kept staring at the floor, fidgeting his fingers, and bouncing one leg up and down. He started to slightly shake his head no, as if every ounce of his body wanted—or needed—to let the truth out, but his mind was not cooperating. I felt as though I was witnessing an internal struggle, one that could not have been prompted just by that one word I had finally managed to voice.

No, I knew Alex. I knew that something was hurting him deep inside. Was the reason why he had cheated really *that* bad? *Oh my gosh*, I thought, *what if the worst had yet to come?* But what could be worse than him cheating on me and breaking our family? I placed my hands on the bed and grabbed the sheets, ready to brace myself for impact.

"Alex?" I whispered.

"I . . ." he kept shaking his head no. "I . . ."

I held my breath.

"I was sexually abused as a child," he blurted out all at once. Then he let out the loudest, most painful cry I had ever heard in my entire life. It reminded me of the cry of a wounded and dying animal.

What?

"What?" I voiced my thought. That made no sense. I had known Alex since we were both teenagers, and never once had he mentioned or led me to believe that he had experienced anything less than a healthy, normal childhood. Sure, he moved often because of his family and their business—going back and forth to Italy—but other than that, he had a solid life at home. Or so I'd thought.

"I was sexually assaulted as a child," he repeated.

Oh my God.

What was I supposed to do? Was I supposed to go and hug him and tell him everything was going to be okay? Or was I supposed to shout at him because that didn't explain why he cheated on me? I looked around the room as if it held the right answer. But there was nothing.

"Who?" I don't know why I asked that question and didn't even know it was coming until I heard my own voice.

Alex sighed heavily, trying hard to control his breathing. He shook his head, squeezed his eyes shut as if to erase whatever mental picture he had just seen pop up in his mind, and said, "A family friend."

"Oh my God . . ." I couldn't fathom it. A family friend? Immediately, a storm of questions thundered through my mind: Did we share Thanksgiving meals with this person?

Did we exchange gifts during the holidays? Did we take family photos together? Oh my God! A cold shiver ran down my spine so fast it jolted me to sit up straight. Alex had hidden his face in his hands but was still crying. Sobbing, actually.

"I'm sor—" but the last bit of that word died in my throat. Was I sorry? Yes, of course I was. My beloved husband had experienced something so awful, and he was still clearly suffering from it. But I wanted to punch him in the face because he had chosen *this* time to share this horror. I just couldn't understand. I had just found out that he had been cheating on me with this woman for the past two months, and now, on top of that hard pill to swallow, I was supposed to also take in another one?

"What the hell, Alex?" I exploded.

He looked at me, his eyes wide with surprise at the unexpected burst.

"You son of a bitch!" I said, getting up from the bed. "First, you tell me you cheated on me, and then, as if to cover your ass and make me pity you, you tell me you were abused? And now, what am I supposed to do? If I stand here and give you what you deserve, I feel like a horrible person because it seems I don't care about your childhood trauma." I began pacing around the room, back and forth, back and forth. I could feel Alex's gaze follow my movements. "You've had close to three decades to tell me about the abuse—*three decades*, Alex! And you chose *this* moment? Well played, you bastard!"

"Gina—" Alex said, but I interrupted him.

"Don't you dare add anything else," I yelled. "You cheated on me. I'm not going to give you a free pass because you were abused. You hear me?"

Alex remained silent as his eyes returned to the floor.

I felt as though I was fuming out of my nose. I sat back down on the bed, forcing myself away from Alex as I felt the urge to slap him across the face.

We sat there in silence for quite a while, crushed under the weight of these hidden truths.

As my heart rate slowed down and my breathing was back under control, I started thinking a bit more clearly about what had just happened. I had so many questions I wanted to ask Alex but didn't even know where to begin.

I wanted to know if he still kept a relationship with his family friend, why he had decided to cheat on me, and why he had chosen that person. Ugh, so many questions.

But I also realized I was not emotionally ready to handle the answers, so I chose to remain silent. I didn't know if I would ever be strong enough to ask them, and that thought brought on such sadness.

This was my reality now. In a blink of an eye, we went from being a happy and united family having a great time in Mexico to being a broken family dealing with two very painful and deep wounds: sexual abuse and adultery. Were we ever going to recover from either one?

The silence continued until Alex, who had been crying quietly, dried his tears with his shirt, stood up from his chair, and looked at me for the first time.

"We will get through this," he whispered. "I promise you."

At that moment, I felt as though I had been punched in the stomach. I folded over in pain and grabbed onto my belly as if pleading for the pain to stop.

"Gina?" I heard Alex say, although I couldn't see him because my eyes were shut. "Are you okay?"

Am I okay? I screamed inside of me.

Nausea took over me, and I somehow managed to rush to the bathroom, shutting the door behind me. I bent over the toilet and vomited the poison Alex had suddenly brought into my life.

Am I okay? His question pounded in my head.

No, I'm not okay! I wanted to yell at him and then punch *him* in the stomach.

"Gina, can I come in?" he asked.

"No!" I said as I sat down on the floor and flushed the toilet. Then, I took some toilet paper and cleaned my mouth. "This is all your fault!"

He didn't say a word.

"You ruined us!" I shouted.

Still nothing.

"How could you do something like this?" I screamed. "Why would you ever—"

The poison came back up again, this time with so much violence that I feared I would see my own blood mixed in it.

I pounded my fist on the cold, hard floor as I kept on expelling my grief.

By the time my body was done, I felt as though I had no fight left in me. It was difficult to breathe because of how fatigued I was. I was sweating but shivering for how cold I was at the same time. I closed my eyes and plopped my arms to the side of my body, my palms facing upward. At that moment, all I could do was pray silently.

God, please give me the strength to face this. I can't do this without you.

A knock on the door jolted me.

"Gina," Alex whispered. "Can I please come in now?"

I didn't answer. I didn't have the strength for it.

"Gina?" he said, knocking on the door again. "I'm coming in, okay? I'm getting worried because you're not answering."

Alex opened the door and saw me in my misery. I hated him, but something inside me was satisfied that he had witnessed the damage he had done to me. He kneeled close to me and helped me clean my face. I wanted to spit in his.

"I'm going to fix this," he said again.

I clenched my jaw and looked him dead in the eyes.

"I promise," he said, swallowing hard.

Alex helped me get up, and I washed my face—the last thing I needed was for the girls to see that my eyes were red and puffy from crying.

Alex must have been relieved because he expelled a heavy sigh and said, "Why don't we go see the girls? Maybe some fresh air will do you good. They're at the beach—they said they'd be working on their tan after breakfast."

I knew I would have to really hide behind a mask to make sure the girls didn't become suspicious. The last thing I needed was for them to find out what had just happened to our family.

I couldn't let them; they would be devastated, and at their age, I was afraid it would mark their childhood—which, up until that point, had been nothing but idyllic, with Alex and I doing our best to spend quality time with them. I was the adult and had to protect them. So, I looked at myself in the mirror and took a deep breath. My lungs hurt, but I did it.

Without responding to Alex, I took a quick shower—I had yet to change out of my workout clothes, which were basically glued to my skin by then—I put my bathing suit on and walked with Alex to the beach, where sure enough, our three beauties were soaking up the Mexican sun.

"About time, you two!" Bella scolded us. "What took you so long?"

Alex gently placed a beach towel on a vacant lounge chair for me, a gesture I welcomed because I felt lightheaded. I didn't know if that feeling was the result of what had just happened between us or if it was because of the sharp change in temperature—our room had the air conditioning on full blast and at the lowest temperature possible, which was 69 degrees, meaning there was a difference of at least 20 degrees with the outside temperature.

"Mom, are you coming in the water?" Olivia asked.

I looked up at her and saw that her sisters were walking toward the ocean.

"Not right now, Liv," I said, trying to sound as cheerful and normal as possible. "Maybe later."

"Okay," she said before joining Julia and Bella. Thank goodness my daughters were behaving like perfect teenagers: too absorbed in their own world to notice that something was off in mine. I watched them as they dared each other to be the first one to get in the water, promising various punishments to the one who'd be the last one to be fully immersed.

"The last one to get in the water has to be on bathroom cleaning duty for a whole week!" said Julia.

"No, she has to post the most embarrassing photo of herself on Instagram," countered Bella.

Olivia saw her sisters' moves and answered by raising the stakes even more. "Or dance at the resort club tonight. In front of everybody!" she said, enunciating every syllable of that last word.

As I watched their interaction and overheard the terms and conditions of their challenge, I couldn't help but smile at the fact that they were all still basically ashore. The water must have been pretty chilly for them to have to buy themselves time with dares.

"Yes, hello, I would like to make an appointment with a marriage counselor, please," I heard Alex say, so I immediately turned toward him. He was sitting on the lounge chair next to me, phone in hand and firmly placed by his right ear.

His words brought me back to reality. I felt as those I was frozen in place. He had cheated on me, and now our marriage was in trouble. To top it all off, he had just revealed a decades-long secret, one that made me sick to my stomach, especially as I watched my daughters laugh out loud and splash each other.

"I need the first appointment available, please," Alex continued.

I looked at him, and I have to admit that his sense of urgency was reassuring. I couldn't help but think that he must have really wanted to fix our marriage and must have been truly sorry for what he had done. Otherwise, why go through the hassle of scheduling a therapy session back in Albany when you could be enjoying the beach in Cancún?

"Does Friday at five o'clock in the afternoon work for you?" he asked me, placing his hand over the phone, which was still close to his ear.

Did I have any plans for that day? I couldn't even remember.

What day is it today? Oh, yeah, Monday, July 3.

We would be flying back home on Thursday, which meant we would have barely any time to rest before therapy. But we needed to start our recovery somewhere. So, whatever plans I had previously made for Friday afternoon would have to wait. Our marriage was in jeopardy and healing it had to be a priority for both of us.

I nodded yes.

Alex confirmed the appointment, thanked the receptionist, and hung up. He then placed his phone on the small table between us. I glanced at it and saw that the picture of our daughters he used as his wallpaper was still there. I felt somewhat relieved but couldn't pinpoint why exactly.

"Would you like anything to drink?" he asked as he saw a waiter walking toward us.

I shook my head no. Just the thought of fruity drinks made me nauseous. As a matter of fact, my stomach was hurting a bit, and I didn't know if it was because I'd skipped breakfast altogether—with everything that happened, food had been the last thing on my mind—or if it was because of the stress my mind and body had just endured.

Alex sighed heavily and waved the waiter away. The waiter stopped in his tracks, looking every bit surprised that we weren't in the mood for exotic drinks or fun snacks to munch on. After all, we were in paradise, lounging on smooth sand, caressed by the hot sun, and listening to the gentle sound of waves crashing ashore. Who wouldn't want to top off this beautiful day with a mimosa and dried mango bites?

"Maybe later, thank you," Alex added with a smile.

Reassured that we were simply postponing the opportunity to place an order as opposed to dismissing it altogether, the waiter smiled back and wished us a good day before moving on to the next couple who, unlike us, was more than eager to try the margarita of the day—apparently Ambhar Añejo tequila, orange liqueur, and agave nectar with a hint of freshly squeezed lime juice, topped with black-ant salt at the rim. It was ten o'clock in the morning, and although we were in a beautiful and luxurious resort that would make anyone feel tucked away from the rest of the world, I didn't see how that made eating black ants and flushing them down with alcohol a good idea. A closer look at the couple, though, and I understood: they were young, probably honeymooners who still believed that weddings led to happily ever after like in fairytales.

At that moment, I was overcome with conflicting emotions: on one hand, I was jealous of their young love—so perfect, so full of hope—but on the other hand, I was irate and wanted to go yell at them and tell them to enjoy it while it lasted because you can work hard at a marriage for decades and it can still fall apart in a second, crumbling like a sand castle beneath the determined pressure of a wave.

"Mom, Dad, look!" Olivia screamed from the ocean. She was sitting on Julia's shoulders and getting ready to stand up on them as if she was about to perform a tumbling trick at a cheerleading competition.

My heart skipped a beat.

"Don't you even dare," I said out loud, cupping my hands around my mouth to intensify the sound.

I had just barely finished saying these words when Olivia got up on Julia's shoulders, quickly steadied herself while Julia held on to her ankles, and jumped into the water like a seasoned diver. Bella cheered as if her sister had just won a gold medal at the Olympics or something. It all happened so fast that I didn't know if I should be proud of the stunt they had just pulled off or ground their sorry behinds until kingdom come.

"Nice!" Alex clapped but stopped the moment his enthusiastic eyes met my stern stare. "I mean, don't do that. You could get hurt!" he said, adjusting his tone to mirror my concern.

"How?" Bella questioned while Olivia wiped her eyes. "By literally falling into *water*?"

"Don't be a smart aleck," I yelled, sitting up straight.

The girls just gave me a disappointed look that screamed, "Mom, don't be a party pooper."

"It's okay, honey," Alex said, holding my hand and squeezing it.

Instinctively, I pulled my hand away from his. I wasn't ready for physical touch. The small space that separated our lounge chairs was all I could handle at the moment.

"Gina, the girls," he whispered, reminding me that the girls had witnessed my impulsive gesture.

I looked at them and saw that they were staring. They were standing up ashore, one next to the other, and had seen me refuse their father's sweet gesture.

Oh no.

I felt like such a failure. Sure, the girls had witnessed arguments between Alex and me over the years, but nothing major— ever—and I had to make sure that they would never learn what was happening. At least not until I had had a chance to figure out what was going on myself.

I knew they would have questions, and I wanted to make sure I had all the answers before breaking their hearts forever and telling them about what their father had done—if it ever got to that point, of course, which I doubted it would. Not to mention that if it did, I knew I would give Alex a chance to talk to them and own up to what he had done.

Alex took my hand again, and this time, I didn't let go. Instead, I looked at the girls and smiled at them. The gesture must have reassured them as they went back to having fun in the water, often teasing me with more tumbling stunts.

That day, like the rest of the trip, I felt completely out of it while forcing myself to appear plugged in to give our daughters the impression that all was well. But the entire time, I was sick to my stomach. Actually sick. I threw up a lot, even though I was barely eating. Because of the lack of nutrition, I also felt tired and sluggish, so I mostly lounged or rested in bed.

Despite my best efforts, Julia noticed that something was not right, and she soon began spending more time with me, coming into my room to check and see how I was feeling, asking me how my day was, and so forth. While I appreciated her empathy, I felt as though I wanted to push her away because I was afraid I would reveal too much. So, when Bella and Olivia also began to suspect something was off, I came up with what I thought was the best and most believable excuse. "I must have eaten something that didn't agree with me."

There. My girls knew I had been suffering from food intolerance for quite a few years. I had no idea why, but raw carrots and celery—among other things—made me sick. So, I told them a lie and said I'd had some crudités with fresh guacamole on Monday and that it was still giving me stomach issues.

"Mom," Olivia said in a stern and disappointed tone. "You know that eating raw vegetables makes you sick, so why would you eat them? See, you've ruined your vacation now. And all for some fresh guac." She added emphasis by waving her index finger at me.

"Olivia," Alex said. "Don't talk to your mother like that."

"It's okay," I said. "Liv is right. I should have known better."

I spent the entire day in bed, curled up in the fetal position and sobbing on and off; the weight of what had happened during the past few days was pulling me down with a force that felt stronger than gravity.

"Mom," Julia whispered as she slightly opened the door. "Are you awake?" She couldn't tell because all of the blinds were closed. I didn't even want to peek outside.

"Yes, honey," I said. "Are you okay?"

"I am, but you're not," she said, slowly walking to my side of the bed, careful not to bump into any furniture as she felt her way through the dark room. "What's wrong?"

I knew this was a decisive moment. My oldest daughter was close to calling my bluff, and I had to do all I could to divert her attention. We were there for her Sweet 16, and suddenly, I had this image in my head of Julia at my age, thinking back on the birthday celebration that changed her life forever because her parents had decided to divorce.

I couldn't let that happen. I had no control over what Alex did to cause me this pain, but darn it, I *did* have control over the pain my daughters would or would not be feeling.

So, I sat up straight, took her hand, and said, "Everything is fine. I just feel like a bit of a party pooper because I don't feel well, and I've been afraid of ruining your birthday with my stomach issues."

Julia sighed in relief and squeezed my hand. "No, Mom," she said, her voice as sweet as ever. "You could never ruin my birthday. I've had a great time here, and even though I'm sad we have to leave tomorrow, I will never forget how much fun we all had. So, thank you."

And she just about won the award for Best Daughter of the Year when she gave me a kiss on the cheek. Those were hard to come by now that they were all teenagers, and that gesture made me cherish it even more.

"Shall we go to dinner then?" I said, feeling energized by Julia's love and attention.

"Are you feeling well enough?" she asked, standing up.

"Of course!" I said, standing up as well and giving my firstborn a hug.

"Let's go then!" she said, pulling me by the hand.

Our last dinner in Mexico was both fun and delicious— although I could only nibble at the food, as my stomach was still completely shut down. But a live band played beautiful Spanish music, the light breeze from the ocean made the heat feel tolerable, and the girls never stopped smiling. After dinner, the girls went to the resort club while Alex and I went back to our room to start packing, as our flight was scheduled early the next morning.

While packing, Alex and I didn't talk much, as the uncertainty of what would happen once we were back in Albany loomed on the horizon and perhaps scared us both. The few words we did exchange seemed precooked, like those meals you get in the frozen food aisle at the grocery store, like: "The girls sure are growing up fast," "We should come here again sometime," and "The food was delicious." No mention of the affair or abuse. And I was glad because I just couldn't handle it.

Chapter Nine

I opened my eyes and checked my phone sitting on the nightstand. It was six o'clock in the morning. I stretched in bed, feeling every bit sore from another restless night. We had been back home for a little over a week; still, every time I closed my eyes, all I could see was Alex confessing to the adultery. I turned to the side and saw that he was no longer in bed, and judging by the silence coming from our en-suite bathroom, he wasn't taking a shower either.

He must have already left, I thought.

I got out of bed, took a quick shower, and got dressed before heading downstairs to the kitchen.

I was making myself a cup of hot coffee when my phone rang.

"Hey, honey." It was Alex. "How did you sleep last night?"

"I slept okay," I exaggerated. "How about you?"

"Not too bad," he said. I could hear the sound of paper shuffling in the background. "I wanted to call and see how you were doing because I left earlier this morning while you were still asleep."

"It's okay," I said. "How's work?"

"Busy as always," Alex said. "I am trying to make sense of all this paperwork I have to do, but it'll take me a while, even though I was hoping to be done by now, which is why I left at five o'clock this morning."

The coffee maker gurgled. I was still suffering from stomach pains because of the stress, and most of the time, I had to force myself to eat anything, which caused me to lose weight rather quickly. By this point, I had lost eight pounds; it wouldn't be long before people would start to notice, especially because I was already on the smaller side.

"Well, I don't want to keep you," I told him while pouring coffee into my favorite mug—a blue Disney cup with Cinderella's Castle on it.

"I just wanted to hear your voice," Alex said in a lower tone, almost like a whisper. He sounded sincere and sweet. "I'll call you later, okay?"

"Okay," I said, sitting down at the kitchen table.

"I love you," he said.

"Love you too," I said and hung up.

I took a sip of my coffee and, while embracing the cup with both hands, enjoyed the sensation of the hot beverage gently waking my body from the inside out. The house was quiet, mainly because the girls were still asleep. It was six-thirty, and I didn't expect to see them anytime soon.

Be still and know that I am God. (PSALM 46:10 [NIV]) Because it was summertime, they didn't have school or sports in the morning, so they could rest as much as needed.

Since coming back from Mexico, Alex and I had gone to therapy three times. Fortunately, the girls were far too invested in their own teenage drama, fraught with social media posts, friends, and celebrity gossip, to notice.

Sitting there, I couldn't help but feel that we had dodged a major bullet. Sure, the past week had been devastating, and we both had wounds that needed to heal, but judging by Alex's recent behavior and his response to the therapy sessions we had been attending, I couldn't help but be optimistic. Even the therapist thought so. Alex took full responsibility for the pain he had caused me, which the therapist saw as a good sign. Alex was remorseful, understood the damage he had brought into our lives, and was repentant enough to want to fix it.

According to our therapist, Alex was showing every sign of being committed to our marriage, family, and the life we had built together. This was already a huge step forward. The therapist also said that my ability to see that Alex was a good man who had made a stupid mistake had helped me put things in the right perspective, which hopefully meant that we were going to move past this sooner rather than later. I, too, appreciated Alex's commitment, and I could feel the anger I felt toward him slowly dissipating.

Alex also talked about being abused as a child, albeit briefly. The therapist recommended we focus first on the affair and then on the abuse and said that Alex would have to be the one to do the hard work of dealing with his childhood trauma. To make sure Alex could truly focus on healing and feel free to share as much as he needed to, the therapist suggested that he start going to therapy on his

Alex was showing every sign of being committed to our marriage, family, and the life we had built together.

own, in addition to maintaining his commitment to our marriage counseling sessions. I understood and vowed to be there for him in any way I possibly could.

Ping.

A notification on my phone reminded me that I was supposed to confirm the reservation for the house I had found for our Cape Cod getaway next week—a trip I had been planning for the past several months. I clicked *Remind Me Later* so I could finish enjoying my warm coffee, but I couldn't help but smile at the thought of going to this gorgeous and luxurious house I'd seen on VRBO.com a few months prior.

Like every year, we would get together with friends and spend a few days on Cape Cod. Being ten adults and thirteen children—all of them girls—we needed a house big enough to host us all. But it wasn't easy to find one, especially because we also wanted a house that would allow all married couples to have similarly sized bedrooms—otherwise, how would we decide who'd get which room? Year after year, we kept changing houses, hoping to find the perfect one with enough room to entertain such a large group. But there'd been no such luck until a few months ago.

While browsing one of my favorite websites for rental properties, I came across this expansive house by the beach, which offered more than I could have possibly dreamed of. It had a vast living room with multiple couches and armchairs, perfect for big gatherings. The all-white gourmet kitchen with a large island in the middle and marble countertops was perfect for my friends who enjoyed cooking to have a great time—and I could have a great time enjoying the meals they prepared. There were five bedrooms with en-suite bathrooms and many others with bunkbeds for all the girls. Out back, there was an infinity pool with plenty of lounge chairs, a tennis court, and even a large patio with a fire pit for fun chitchats and s'mores.

Like every year, I was the one organizing things. I don't remember how I became the designated planner, but it was a role that I enjoyed and took on without making a fuss. There was just something so exciting about looking at rental properties and clicking through all the photos to see which house might work for us this year. I was also in charge of the grocery list, which was then given to the husbands to run out to Stop and Shop and gather everything needed for the week. Each household would be splitting the costs, so while I was making all the arrangements, I wasn't paying for everything.

Ping.

My phone beeped again. I had been so lost in thought, I hadn't realized a whole hour had gone by since I dismissed the first notification. So, I got up, went to the office, sat down in front of the computer, and paid the confirmation fee—the property was ours. As I looked through the photos one more time, it was hard not to get excited about the amazing time we were about to have.

Life was slowly but surely returning to normal, and I knew in my heart that we were going to go back to being the Gina and Alex all of our friends knew. What I'd found out in Mexico would be a major obstacle in our story but one we would move on from. We were going to have our happily ever after; I was sure of it.

We were going to have our happily ever after; I was sure of it.

"House booked," I texted Alex.

"Awesome, thanks!" he texted back immediately. "Girls up yet?"

"I hear something coming from their bedrooms, so I assume they are," I replied.

"Tell them I love them," Alex wrote.

As always, he was the most attentive father any spouse could ever hope for. I was about to text him back when—

"Hi, Mom."

I turned around and saw Olivia standing behind me. She was still in her pajamas, her hair tied up in a bun.

"Hi, Liv," I greeted her back. "How did you sleep?"

"Okay," she said, rubbing her eyes.

"Are your sisters up as well?" I asked, closing the browser. She nodded yes and yawned.

"What would you like for breakfast?" I asked her as I walked out of the office and headed toward the kitchen.

"Can you make pancakes?" she asked.

"Alright. Do you want them shaped like a heart like when you were little?" I teased her.

"Mommm," she whined.

"Ask Julia and Bella if they want some, too, please," I said. "I don't want to make three different types of breakfast."

Olivia shouted my request at her sisters, who answered with a resounding, "*Yes!*"

Pancakes it was.

Although cooking was not my forte, I had to admit that pancakes were a specialty of mine. My daughters enjoyed the light dusting of cinnamon and the drop or two of pure vanilla extract I added to the batter, which I elevated even further with a pinch of salt. Judging by how fast the girls ate the pancakes, rest or no rest, I could still make mouth-watering pancakes. The sight of my daughters' smiles, glossy and sticky with maple syrup, always brought a genuine sense of joy to my heart.

After breakfast, the girls hung out with their friends at the nearby park, and I went on about my day, which was filled with errands for our trip to Massachusetts. My first stop was the Co-Op—by far, my favorite grocery store where I could find genuinely organic food. I was, and still am, quite health-conscious, so eating a clean diet was a priority for me.

While looking at the fresh fish selection, I spotted some beautiful Atlantic salmon filets, and knowing how much Alex loves salmon, I bought two of them. They had been prepared with a pistachio and coconut crust, which I knew he was going to enjoy.

Next, I dropped off Alex's suit at the dry cleaners. As I was getting back in the car, he called to check on me, which I appreciated because I knew he had been having a busy day.

Then, I made my way to the hair salon, where, aside from getting a fresh blowout, I also got a much-needed mani-pedi. Before leaving, I looked at myself in the mirror and truly liked what I saw—although the dark circles underneath my eyes reminded me that I needed to rest.

That evening, Alex came home around nine o'clock, a bit later than usual, which I expected, as he had been busy all day.

"I was thinking," he said after dinner while we were getting ready for bed, "I want to take another step into our recovery and hold myself accountable even more."

"Oh?" I had no idea what he was referring to.

"I want to tell my sisters about what I did," Alex said.

"What?" I didn't know what to say. On one hand, I felt proud of him because I knew this wouldn't be easy. But on the other hand, I felt so embarrassed. I didn't know if I was ready for family members to know what had happened in our marriage. "Are you sure?"

"Yes," he said. "I thought about it all day, and I think it's the right thing to do."

I smiled at him and decided to follow his lead on this one.

"Should we tell my sister, too, then?" I asked.

"Yes," he said. "We'll call them soon."

With that, we went to bed, but it took me a long time to fall asleep. My heart was pounding at the thought of explaining everything to our sisters. For the first time, somebody close to us would know what had happened, and I feared that telling them, hearing their reaction, would turn this nightmare into a big reality. What were they going to say? Were they going to judge Alex? Would they try to convince me to divorce him? There was just no way I would let them do that to us. The thought of opening up to them about the state of my marriage made me feel so exposed, as if I was being forced to peel off a protective layer I had been hiding behind.

Not my own will, by Thy will be done. (Luke 22:42)

The day before we were supposed to leave for Cape Cod, we called our sisters. One at a time, Alex spoke to them, owning up to his mistake. He reassured them that we were on the mend and that revealing the truth to them was a way for him to help us heal from the damage he had caused.

Our sisters were shocked, to say the least. There were periods of heavy silence, punctuated by trembling voices filled with emotions, and there was one question that kept coming up: "Are you going to be okay?" It was directed at me more than him, but we answered together and promised them we were working hard to heal our wounds.

"Gina, do you need me to come and stay with you for a while?" my sister asked. She had recently moved two hours away, and at that moment, I knew she regretted doing it—had she been any closer, she would have come to my house right away to check and see with her own eyes that I was indeed doing well.

"No, I'm fine," I insisted, doing my best to reassure her.

"Okay . . ." she said.

I knew I hadn't succeeded in convincing her, but once the phone calls were over, I let out a big sigh of relief. Alex smiled at me and kissed my forehead. We'd been holding hands while we were on the phone, and I could tell that we both felt as though a giant rock had been lifted off our shoulders.

The rest of the day went on as usual. The girls went off to see friends, Alex went to work, and I was busy with last-minute planning for Cape Cod. Alex had warned me that, since he had stayed home a bit later that morning to make the calls to our siblings, he would be late coming back that evening. But it was now ten o'clock at night, and he had yet to return. Worried, I called him.

His phone rang, but he didn't pick up.

I called him again.

Nothing.

I was about to text him when I saw he was calling me back.

"Hey, are you okay?" I asked him right away.

"Gina," he said, his tone somber.

Immediately, my heart stopped beating. Had Alex been in an accident? Was he calling me from the hospital?

"Alex?" My hands were shaking with anxiety. I knew that whatever he was about to say, it was not going to be good news.

"I'm not coming home tonight," he said. "I'm staying at a hotel." I could tell he had been crying because his voice trembled.

I froze.

Before I could ask him why, he said, "Gina, I lied when I said I had only been seeing her for a couple of months. The truth is, I have been with her for the past two years." He paused. "I think I love her."

Chapter Ten

"I am going to move out," Alex said while sitting in my car. He had called soon after our conversation and asked me to meet him at the local Fresh Market parking lot—at four o'clock in the morning. Fortunately, my sister-in-law had come quickly to the house to look after the girls when I called her in tears earlier, telling her Alex had confessed to being in love with the other woman.

I thought Alex wanted to meet with me because he wanted to apologize and find a way to fix the mess he had created. I was certainly not expecting him to tell me he wanted to move out. I felt empty inside. It was as if my body had become a shell, and I could not hear a sound around me. I felt completely and utterly alone. I needed God more than ever and knew

> He performs wonders that cannot be fathomed, miracles that cannot be counted.
> (Job 5:9)

praying would be the only way to fix us. Through God, miracles happen. And we needed a miracle.

I looked at him in silence.

"Gina," he said. "I *am* going to move out." As if I needed to hear those words again.

"Get the hell out of my car!" I said, grinding my teeth.

As soon as he shut the door and got back into his car in the Fresh Market parking lot, I drove home. But his confession of his presumed love for that other woman and that he had been seeing her for years echoed in my head like an inescapable torture.

This couldn't be my life. This couldn't be my marriage. This couldn't be us.

I don't remember driving home, but suddenly, I found myself sitting in the kitchen with a warm cup of coffee in front of me, staring into nothing. The sun wasn't even up yet, and I hadn't turned the lights on. Something about being surrounded by darkness brought me comfort.

I think I love her . . .

I punched my fist on the table.

I wanted his voice out of my head and squeezed my eyes shut as if trying to delete the memory, even though I knew it was futile.

"Hey, Mom." Julia startled me as she entered the kitchen and turned on the light. "What are you doing here in the dark?"

"Oh," I didn't know what to say. "Um . . . I didn't want to wake you all up."

"Oh-kay . . ." Julia said, and even though I couldn't see her because I was temporarily blinded by the bright light, I could sense she had just rolled her eyes at my odd behavior. "Is everything alright?" she asked.

No. Your father has been having an affair and has decided to destroy us.

"Yes," I lied. "Of course."

"Okay," she said, "I'm going to get ready for Cape Cod."

Oh no! Cape Cod!

I had forgotten all about the trip we were supposed to be going to go on in a few hours. I really was not in the right headspace for a week of socializing at the beach, nor for seeing Alex again so quickly (although he would be coming a day later). All I wanted to do was crawl up in bed and cry. But canceling this trip at the last minute—a trip we had taken every year—was a sure way to raise a major red flag to the girls and all of our friends, which would spark a long list of questions to ensure everything was fine in my life.

At that moment, I had less energy to deal with an inquisition than I did with loading up the car and driving there with my girls. So, I got up, took a shower, and got ready for our family vacation.

The drive to Cape Cod was uneventful, thank goodness—especially because I found it hard to focus on driving when my mind felt as though it was stuck in a whirlwind. Fortunately, Alex wasn't supposed to come with us because he was at a men's retreat in Upstate New York, a trip he had scheduled not long after we were back from Mexico. This retreat was all about blowing off steam and doing "manly activities," whatever that meant. Supposedly, it was a way for him to show me he wanted to fix our marriage, or so he had told me—before his big love confession a few hours prior.

The good thing about Alex not being in the car was, of course, I didn't have to deal with his presence. I didn't have to put up a façade of what a blissful marriage we had in front of the girls—who knew their father was away at a retreat but didn't know the real reason why he had decided to attend it.

Once we got to the house, the girls ran inside to meet their friends and left me alone to unload the car—not that I was surprised; they were three teenage girls who were always lost in their own world and seemed oblivious to the rest of us. I grabbed their luggage from the trunk when I heard, "Well, you look wicked thin!"

"Hi, Gwen," I said, looking up at my longtime friend who was walking toward me from the house. "How are you? You look great in that white and blue sundress!"

"Oh, stop it," she said, helping me cart the luggage to the house. "But I want to know the diet you're on because the last time I saw you—and it was only a couple of weeks ago—you didn't look this thin! What's going on? Are you doing okay?"

"Of course," I said, forcing a smile. "Everything is fine."

"Is Alex at the retreat then?" she asked as she opened the front door to let me in.

"Yeah," I said. "He'll be here tomorrow." I did my best to sound nonchalant about it so as not to raise suspicion.

Once I entered the house—which was more majestic than I thought, as the pictures clearly didn't do it justice— other friends came to greet me and help me bring the luggage to our bedrooms. They all let me know they had noticed I'd lost weight, which I did my best to brush off with an "Oh, I've just been having some stomach problems lately, that's all."

Some of the husbands bought what I said, while the ladies—Laurie, Gwen, Vicki, and Nancy—gave me a raised-eyebrow look, letting me know they felt something else was going on. I replied to their silent remarks with a smile and walked upstairs to unpack my luggage.

The bedroom was spacious and stunning: it had a king bed with a beautiful white frame that perfectly matched the white nightstands and dresser. Light blue lamps accentuated the room, and a large painting of a sailboat in choppy waters gave off a genuine Cape Cod vibe.

As I placed my clothes in the drawers of the long dresser, I could hear my girls laughing and giggling with their friends as they ran through the halls of the second floor. Something about how carefree and genuinely happy they sounded brought tears to my eyes because they would eventually have to learn what was truly going on between their dad and me.

At the thought of my daughters finding out what their dad did, my legs suddenly felt extremely weak, and I fell to my knees and hid my face in my hands, sobbing. This was my reality now, my family. My broken family. My life went from being a bad situation to a horrible nightmare within a week.

One moment, I thought Alex and I were going to work on our marriage together because we both wanted to fix it and move on. The next, he told me he was in love with her, wanted to move out, and now our family was broken.

The more I cried, the more my stomach hurt. I placed my hands on it, begging it to stop cramping. It was so painful that I folded over in agony.

After taking a few deep breaths, I was able to calm down. As I pulled myself up from the floor and sat on the bed, I tried to remind myself that I could no longer look at the bigger picture: I had to take life one moment at a time because a moment was all I could handle. Looking at the bigger picture was only going to scare me and bring me back to my knees. I had to focus on the here and now.

So, I went to the bathroom—which had a stylish marble countertop—to wash my face and touch up my makeup.

Once I was sure nobody could tell I had been crying, I went back downstairs.

It was a relief to see that my friends had already put the groceries away as if they had sensed I needed help—even though they weren't sure what was going on or what I needed help with. For the rest of the day, none of them asked me how I was doing, and I certainly appreciated their efforts not to make me feel under the spotlight.

I genuinely enjoyed our first day in Cape Cod. We made prosciutto and mortadella sandwiches, prepared a healthy and refreshing fruit salad, and packed the coolers and bags for lunch on the beach—we had arrived in Cape Cod right before lunchtime. After putting on our bathing suits, we walked toward the water through our private access and lounged there the entire day, constantly snacking—there is just something about going to the beach that makes you feel like you're always hungry!

Gwen, Laurie, Vicki, Nancy, and I lounged and sunbathed while our daughters splashed each other in the sea and raced one another to see who could swim faster and farther. Meanwhile, their husbands played pool in the game room.

"Gina," Laurie said, "have you heard of the musical the girls are working on?"

Our daughters all attended the same private Catholic, all-girls school in Upstate New York, and Laurie was the head of the Friends of the Arts, so she was always at the rehearsals.

"Yes," I said, not really sure why she had brought it up.

"Well, let me tell you about the auditions," she said. "I, for one, am not that happy with the process because . . ."

I think I love her.

Alex's words suddenly slapped me across the face so hard they took my breath away. I was just lounging with my girlfriends and having a good time, reassured by how much fun my daughters were having, so I was certainly not expecting to experience that flashback.

My body was shaking from the inside out, and I felt the urge to get up and run to my room, curl up in a ball, and cry my heart out. Reality had spit in my face. Thank goodness Alex was not there, or I don't think I could have handled being in his presence. But I knew I had to pull it together because, whether or not I was ready for it, Alex was going to join us in Cape Cod the very next day, and I had to prepare myself for the possibility of experiencing another flashback and, this time, in his presence.

I am at the beach, I told myself, as I placed my right foot on the warm sand to ground me even more. *I feel the sun on my skin.* I closed my eyes to focus on how warm my skin felt. *I hear my daughters laughing.* I took deep, regular breaths as I smiled at their loud giggles. *I taste the salt water on my lips.* This exercise helped me focus on the here and now, and I felt as though I no longer had a crushing weight on my chest.

"Do you agree?" Laurie asked, making me open my eyes—which I did slowly to welcome the sunlight—and realize I had completely missed her speech on the new musical and why she wasn't happy about the audition process.

Unsure of what to say and attempting not to raise any suspicion that I had not listened to a word of it, I just nodded yes. Fortunately, Laurie changed the subject by inviting us all to go for a swim.

"I'll join you soon," I said, feeling the need to be alone for a moment. I hadn't slept much—if at all—the night before, and the weakness I felt in my body was a sign of how desperately I needed to rest. But I couldn't silence my brain. Whenever I closed my eyes, horrible images of what

Alex had done haunted me. I shook my head to try to get rid of them, but it was futile. Was I ever going to be happy again? Was I ever going to put this mess behind me? Was I ever going to recover from this? Too many thoughts crowded my head, too many questions scared my heart.

I opened my eyes again and saw my friends walking to the shore, where they were splashed by our daughters, who,

Was I ever going to be happy again?

feeling bold and brave, thought it was a good idea to get the grownups wet before they were ready to be. I could tell by looking at my friends' faces—and their menacing grins—that there would be hell to pay later at the house for our girls, which most likely meant they were going to be on dishwashing duty. I smiled, feeling reassured by the predictability of it all.

I heard familiar voices coming from the house, and when I looked back toward them, I saw that my girlfriends' husbands were walking to the beach to join us. Alex was the only one missing. I took another deep breath and felt an overwhelming sense of positivity wash over me. He was at the retreat, and I couldn't help but hope that whatever they were doing there would give him the clarity to understand our marriage and family were worth saving.

I closed my eyes and prayed that tomorrow he would come and tell me that this retreat had been such a revelatory experience for him, that he had understood I am the only woman he has and will ever love, and he wanted to do all he could to make our marriage go back to the blissful state we once had.

I opened my eyes again and saw a big smile on my daughters' faces as they played in the water. Yes, the road ahead of us would be bumpy, but as long as Alex was committed to saving our marriage, I knew nothing could stop us. With a renewed sense of hope, I got up and walked toward my friends and daughters. The cool ocean water welcomed me with a splash, inviting me to let myself go, if only just for a swim.

Chapter Eleven

"**A**re you not hungry?" Gwen asked me at dinner at the Wild Goose Tavern in Chatham, a charming seaside town in southeast Cape Cod.

I looked at the food galore in front of me: goose lobster bisque, jumbo shrimp cocktail, charcuterie board with their scrumptious house-made smoked bluefish pate, honey-baked smoked salmon, flatbread crackers, and caperberries. As inviting as it all seemed and as delicious as it smelled, my stomach was in knots.

I shook my head no, smiling at her.

Her eyes lingered on me as if to acknowledge that she suspected something was off, but she was not going to pry.

I was sitting next to her husband, Paul, who had been close friends with Alex for many years.

"So, Alex comes back tomorrow from the retreat, huh?" Paul asked as he enjoyed another spoonful of his curry seafood stew. The coconut curry sauce added a fragrant and exotic smell to the atmosphere, a smell I found appealing and soothing.

"Ehm, yes, tomorrow," I mumbled.

I took a few flatbread crackers and began munching on them to avoid raising suspicion about if and how much I ate. I glanced at everybody else at the table and could tell they were all having a great time. Julia, Bella, and Olivia were chatting away with their friends while Laurie, Vicki, and Nancy were talking up a storm about who knows what. Since everybody was talking, voices mixed, and so did words, entangled in a loud vortex of chatter that made me feel at ease and not on the spot.

"Paul," I said, leaning closer to him. "When we go back to the house, can I talk to you?"

Gwen heard and looked at her husband.

"Of course," he said. "Is everything okay?"

I didn't answer. Instead, I just looked at him and Gwen, who nodded knowingly.

Later that evening, after we had returned to the house and everybody was making their way to their bedrooms, I walked over to Gwen and Paul's room. It was above the garage in front of the main house, which offered the privacy I felt I needed to have that conversation.

Gwen and Paul had been through something similar to what Alex and I were going through. They had separated for a while and then reconciled. I knew they could help me figure out what to do next and how Alex and I could find our way back to a loving marriage.

"Sit down," Gwen said when I walked into their room.

I took a seat in one of the comfortable armchairs that were placed around a rectangular coffee table in what looked to be a small yet inviting living room in their open-concept bedroom.

"What's going on?" Paul asked.

I took a deep breath, closed my eyes, and revealed, "Alex has had an affair and wants to move out."

At the sound of my own voice uttering what was now my reality, I burst into tears. Gwen gasped and placed both hands over her mouth, which was open with shock. Paul leaned back in his armchair, his arms draped over the sides.

There would have been complete silence if not for my sobbing.

After a while, Paul said, "You and Alex can get through this."

"Yes," Gwen echoed. "We did, and so will you." She placed her hand on mine and smiled.

I dried my tears and said, "I just don't know what to do. I hope this retreat clears his head, and when he gets here tomorrow, he'll say he wants to work on our marriage . . . the last thing Alex said to me was that he thought he was in love with her and wanted to move out."

That revelation prompted even more tears to come out.

"Listen," Paul said, "he's extremely confused now, but trust me, he'll get back to his senses. Why don't you and Alex come to our church?"

"That's how we saved our marriage," Gwen said, still holding my hand. "We found God, and through Him, we worked on us."

"I'd like that," I said, drying my tears with the palm of my hand. "I don't know if Alex would be open to it, though. **We found God, and through Him, we worked on us.**

He's been kind of wary of church lately."

"Let me talk to him," Paul said as Gwen offered me tissues. "Why don't I go pick him up at the airport tomorrow? I can take him to lunch, and we can talk about this whole situation. Trust me, he'll listen to me, not only because I'm his friend, but also because I've been through it before and know how he feels."

I nodded in agreement.

"It'll be okay," Gwen whispered.

"I just don't want anyone else to know," I said, drying my eyes again. "The girls don't know anything, and I don't know how I am going to tell them yet."

"We won't say a word," Gwen reassured me. "But if I can give you a piece of advice, it's that our children are more sensitive than we think. They might not know all the details but can tell there's something wrong with their parents. They pick up on the energy, so don't be surprised if they just come and ask you out of the blue."

I knew she was right. The thought that my girls were going to find out the truth sooner than I wanted them to made my stomach turn on itself, causing me to feel nauseous and dizzy. I spent a few more minutes with Gwen and Paul as they reassured me that they were going to do all they could to help me and my family through this tough time. Then, I wished them goodnight and walked back to my bedroom.

The house was quiet. Everybody was asleep. The first day in Cape Cod had been a lot of fun for everybody, especially my girls. For that, I was truly thankful. I wanted them to have fun and be as carefree as they possibly could, especially because I knew what was on the horizon for them. I asked God to show me what to do, tell me what to say, take me where I should be. I looked for signs from Him everywhere—in the sunrise, a beautiful flower, or the time on the clock. ANYTHING to show me He was with me.

After taking a hot shower, I went to bed. But I couldn't sleep. Instead, I stared at the ceiling as thoughts of Alex, his affair, and our future crowded my mind and shattered my heart. More tears followed as I hugged the extra pillow next to me and soaked it in pain and betrayal. Eventually, sleep welcomed me into its comforting arms, if only for a few hours.

The next morning, I woke up to the sound of laughter and chatter. I quickly recognized my daughters' giggles as I slowly opened my eyes. Their happiness was the medicine my heart needed to not fall apart completely. I decided to remain in bed for a few more minutes and attempt to mentally and emotionally prepare myself for the day ahead. Alex would arrive later that morning, and we would have to find a way to coexist without letting anybody suspect anything was wrong.

I think I love her . . .

I placed my hands over my ears and closed my eyes shut. I didn't want to hear those words ever again.

"Ugh!" I released an exasperated sigh and got up.

He's more than likely come to his senses, I thought as I got dressed. *That retreat surely refocused his mind on what truly mattered in his life.* I couldn't help but feel positive that he would tell me he no longer wanted to move out. Sure, we had a lot of work ahead of us, but I knew we could do it. Paul would talk to him this morning and encourage him to go to church so we could begin healing from this setback.

I walked into the bathroom, brushed my hair, and put on some Chapstick to prevent the sun from drying my lips. I looked at myself in the mirror, and, despite being thinner than usual and my eyes conveying just how tired I was, I was proud of who I saw: a resilient woman in a light blue sundress who had just been dealt a curveball that could have easily knocked her out completely. Yet, she became even more determined not to give up.

GINA TRONCO

I walked downstairs as the sweet smell of pancakes and the sound of crackling bacon welcomed me.

I was proud of the resilient woman I was.

"Morning, everyone," I said as I entered the kitchen where the long dining room table was. Gwen, Laurie, Vicki, and Nancy were busy flipping pancakes, peeling and cutting fresh fruit, and cooking bacon while their husbands were outside enjoying coffee.

"Hi, Mom," Julia said, sitting with her sisters and friends at the table. "How did you sleep?"

"I slept okay," I said as I sat in the empty chair next to her. "You?"

"Like a rock!" she said.

"When's Dad coming?" Olivia asked before biting into her three pancakes that were neatly stacked, one on top of the other on her plate.

"Later today," I said. "Uncle Paul is going to pick him up and take him out to lunch. Then they'll be on their way here."

"Okay," she said.

"Are you going to have any breakfast?" Julia asked.

"Maybe later," I said.

"You haven't been eating much—if at all—lately," she said, her tone lowering as if to make sure her sisters sitting across from us wouldn't hear her comment. Fortunately, it seemed to have worked because both Olivia and Bella continued to eat their breakfast while listening to their friends plan the day. Judging by what I overheard, there was a whole lot of sunbathing involved.

"Mom?" Julia asked for my attention.

"I'm fine," I said, smiling. "I just have been having some stomach issues, that's all."

"It's been going on for quite a while now," she whispered. "Since we went to Mexico."

Oh no, I thought. *She has been keeping a close eye on me.*

"Everything is fine," I said, placing my hand on her back to reassure her. "Don't worry about me. Just think about having fun."

"Yeah yeah," she said in a singsong tone.

I got up and walked over to the kitchen to grab a plate and fill it with food, with the hope that Julia, seeing that I was indeed having breakfast, would stop worrying about me. My stomach cramped at the mere thought of eating, but I knew I had to force myself to ingest something if I wanted to help my daughter.

I sat down again beside her and began cutting the pancake I had topped with non-fat Greek yogurt, fresh strawberries, and shaved almonds.

"Ready?" Bella said to her friends and sisters, pushing the chair back and getting up.

"Yep!" they all answered in unison.

"Don't forget to clean up after yourselves," I said.

They grabbed their empty plates and put them in the sink. Then they all went to their bedrooms to get ready for the beach.

After they left, I released a sigh of relief because, after taking a few bites of the pancake, I felt full and knew that I could not possibly have any more of it—unless I wanted to spend the next few hours coming and going from the bathroom.

"You okay?" Gwen asked as I brought my plate to the kitchen sink.

"Yeah," I said, offering a smile.

"Paul's leaving for the airport soon," she whispered.

"Thank you," I said. "Do you need any help with that?" I tipped my chin to the last batch of pancakes she was getting ready to cook.

"Nah, we're fine," she said. "Why don't you go and relax?"

"No, no," I insisted. "I am no more of a guest here than you are." I began washing dishes.

"Alright," Paul announced as he walked into the kitchen. "I'm on my way to get Alex."

"Oh good, good!" Laurie said as she grabbed a cup of coffee and walked toward the pool to join her husband. "Glad we'll all be together soon."

"Thank you, Paul," I told him.

He nodded. "I'll be back later," he said, kissing Gwen goodbye.

"Drive safe," she told him as he left the house.

I turned toward the sink again and looked down at the pile of dishes that needed to be scrubbed—the girls had used a lot of maple syrup—before I could put them in the dishwasher. I felt like somebody was squeezing my chest, making it hard for me to breathe. Alex would be joining us on vacation soon, and all I could do was hope he had changed his mind about moving out. The more I thought of what-if scenarios—what if he still wants to move out, what if he is indeed in love with her, what if our family will never be whole again—the more I felt as though the room was spinning and the floor beneath my feet was crumbling.

"Beach?" Gwen asked me.

"Huh?" I looked at her as I placed the last dish in the dishwasher. "Yes, sure . . ."

"You will get through this," she whispered, placing her hand on my shoulder.

I offered a faint smile. "I'll go get ready," I said and walked to my room to change into my bathing suit. After applying sunscreen and more Chapstick, I joined the girls at the beach.

The light breeze coming from the sea was reinvigorating. Even though my friends kept chitchatting with me about this and that, and my daughters were having a lot of fun playing with the other girls, I kept checking the time on my phone.

It's 10:30. Alex should be on the airplane.

I would then place the phone back in my beach bag, look out at the calm sea, and then, without even consciously thinking about it, I would pick up the phone again to check the time, only to realize that only three or four minutes had gone by.

Still on the plane. I thought. *It's just 10:55.*

A few more minutes would go by, and I would check again.

It's 11:25. Alex should have landed by now.

But he hadn't sent me any messages to inform me how the flight had gone like he normally would have.

Yet one more thing that has changed between us.

"Gina," Gwen said, distracting me from my thoughts. "Paul said that he and Alex are in the car and going to the restaurant."

"Oh, thank you." I let out a sigh of relief. I internally prayed: *God, give me the wisdom and strength I need to get through this.*

The rest of the morning and early afternoon were a blur to me. I checked my phone so often that I nearly drained the battery. Finally, around midafternoon, I heard a familiar voice, which made me stand up from my lounge chair right away.

"Hey, everyone."

"Dad!" the girls shouted in unison as they ran toward Alex, who was walking to the beach.

"Hey, slow down," he said with a smile. "You're going to get me all wet."

The girls hugged him even though they were soaked—having just gotten out of the sea.

"How was your flight?" Bella asked him.

"It was good," he said.

I stood there without moving, feet on the warm sand, looking at Alex and the girls. It was as if I was paralyzed.

What should I do? I thought. *Should I go and hug him like I normally would so nobody will suspect anything? What if he doesn't want me to hug him? Do I even want to give him a hug after what he said to me?*

Soon, I saw Paul walking toward Gwen. I stared at him to see if I could read his expression for any positive signs that his conversation with Alex had resulted in my husband coming to his senses. But as soon as he noticed I was looking at him, he briefly met my glance and then looked down as if he couldn't bear to look me in the eyes.

Oh my God . . . What happened? Did Paul not succeed in knocking some sense into Alex? Did he not convince him to go to church to repair our marriage?

Before I could answer any of these questions, I saw Alex walking toward me.

My heart was beating so fast I swear I thought it was going to jump out of my chest. I glanced at Paul, who, taking Gwen by the hand, walked back to the house, whispering something to her.

What do they know that I don't?

"Hi," Alex said to me, bringing my focus back on him.

"Hi," I said, forcing the sound out of my throat.

"How are you?" he asked.

At that moment, I felt the urge to slap him across the face. *How do you think I'm doing?* I screamed in my head. *I'm deteriorating from the inside out because of you! This anxiety, the not knowing what is going to happen to me, to us, is consuming me. I can't deal with you going back and forth on your decisions anymore: one moment, you condemn your own affair, then the next, you confess to wanting to move out.*

I forced a smile as a reply.

"Can you come and help me unpack my bag?" Alex said, but I knew what he meant. He wanted to talk to me and used the unpacking as an excuse to get away from Laurie, Nancy, Vicki, their husbands, and our girls.

I nodded yes and walked back to the house with him.

Once we were in the living room, he grabbed his luggage, which he had momentarily placed next to the couches, and we walked upstairs together. I showed him which bedroom was ours.

"How was the retreat?" I asked him.

"It was good," Alex said, sitting on the bed. "I think it helped me clear my head."

At the sound of his words, I felt as though a huge weight had been lifted off my shoulders. I knew it meant that he had realized the big mistake he was about to make if he indeed moved out.

"I'm so glad to hear that," I said, sitting next to him. "I was hoping it would, and I know that Paul talked to you. I hope you're not upset that I told him and Gwen, but since they've been through something similar before—"

"Gina," he interrupted me, looking down at the floor.

"I know, I should have asked if it was okay with you that they knew, but you were at the retreat, and I didn't want to disturb you—"

"Gina," he interrupted me again, still staring down.

Silence fell upon us.

"I . . ." he began. "I've decided that I am still going to move out."

No.

I couldn't move. Time stood still. The reality of my broken marriage engulfed me.

"I'm sorry," he said, still staring at his damn feet. "I just really need to figure things out and process my feelings, so I need time . . ."

Alex continued talking, but his voice sounded muffled to me, like when you're underwater and can't really hear what anybody else is saying to you.

What the hell did he go to the retreat for? I shouted in my mind.

Suddenly, I felt nauseous. Not physically, but emotionally. I wanted nothing to do with Alex. Even his mere presence—especially the fact that he was sitting right next to me on the bed I slept on—disgusted me. My breathing became more and more intense. I felt like I was on the verge of hyperventilating as his muffled words echoed in my head.

"Get out!" I said, grinding my teeth.

"What?" he asked.

"Get the hell out of my room!" I said, looking straight at him.

"Gina," Alex said, finally lifting up his eyes to meet mine. "We are going to have to share this room, remember?"

"I can't stand being in the same room as you right now," I told him.

"Well, you're going to have to figure out a way to coexist, at least for this week," he said, standing up in front of me and crossing his arms. "Unless you want the girls to understand that something is wrong."

Oh no . . .

I took a deep breath and, squeezing the white blanket with my hands, I looked at him and said, "No, I don't want them to . . . not until we figure out what is going on."

"Good," Alex said.

"So, when are you moving out?" I asked him, my leg jittering in anticipation.

"When we go back home," he said. "I don't know exactly what day, but I think it'll be sooner rather than later."

I nodded in resignation, even though I wanted to shake my head in anger.

He took a deep breath and walked to the bathroom, our conversation over.

"I am going back to the beach," I said out loud for him to hear me through the closed bathroom door.

"Okay," he answered back. "I'll meet you there."

The sun welcomed me as soon as I walked outside the house, prompting me to shield my eyes with my open hand, even though I was wearing sunglasses. I walked over to the beach.

"Where's Dad?" Julia asked while sunbathing.

"He'll be here soon," I said as I sat down and adjusted on the lounge chair beside hers.

"Why don't you go to the other one over there?" she said, pointing to two empty lounge chairs farther away. "So you and Dad can be close."

It was the obvious thing to do, but it hadn't come naturally to me. Of course, I should have chosen to use the lounge chair next to another empty one instead of using the one next to my daughter. I was so surprised at my unnatural choice that I didn't know what to say.

"Did you and Dad have a fight?" she asked.

"No," I lied. "Why would you say that?"

"Mh," she said, shrugging. "You just have that look."

"What look?" I said, perhaps a little too high-pitched.

"You know . . ." Julia looked at me with a raised eyebrow. "The look you get when you and Dad have an argument."

"I don't have a look," I protested. "See, I'm even going to go to the other lounge chair to wait for Dad." I got up and made my way.

"Alright," Julia said as I was walking away. "But you can't lie to me. I know you had a fight."

I pretended I didn't hear her and placed my towel on one of the empty chairs.

Soon after, Alex walked to the beach and sat next to Julia, who quickly said, "Yep, I was right."

"About what?" I overheard Alex ask her.

"You and Mom had a fight," Julia said, now sitting up with her arms crossed.

"Why would you say that?" Alex asked, his tone high-pitched as well.

"Alex," I called him. "Come sit here by me." I pointed to the empty lounge chair to my right.

He got up and came over.

"Did you tell her anything?" he whispered.

"No," I said, my head turning quickly toward him. "Why would you think that?"

"Because she knows something's wrong," he said, this time his tone a bit higher. "I know you're upset, but I would never want to put our girls in the middle."

"Yeah, well, you should have thought about that before you did what you did," I snapped.

Alex rose abruptly and walked back toward the house.

I sighed and shook my head.

Why did I have to say that? And why would he ever assume I said anything to Julia?

My eyes were lost in the distance. I suddenly realized that in this battle, nobody was ever going to be a winner. We were all losers.

"I knew it," Julia said, her arms crossed on her chest, standing right in front of me. Her downward-curled lips told me she sensed that something was seriously wrong. She could feel this was not a typical argument.

Before I could say anything, she turned around and slowly walked toward her sisters and friends who were having fun in the sea.

"Julia," I called, but she pretended not to hear me.

"Is everything okay?" Laurie asked me.

"Yeah," I said. Then, in an attempt to not give anyone else another chance to ask me anything, I got up and went back to the house as well.

When I entered the bedroom, I found Alex sitting on the armchair by the window, his gaze briefly meeting mine.

"I would never dream of telling the girls anything," I said, my voice choking in my throat, for the big lump of tears I felt was suffocating me.

"I know," he said, his voice almost as choked up as mine. "I'm sorry I said that. This is all my fault."

For a moment, I felt the urge to hug him and reassure him that everything was going to be okay. But then, thoughts and flashbacks of what happened, of what he did, of what he told me he was going to do, crowded my mind and my heart. I said between my teeth, "And yet you're not willing to fix it."

With eyes widened with shock at my answer, Alex scoffed and got up, pacing the room back and forth.

"You know what, Gina?" he said. "I'm trying!"

"No, you're not!" I yelled all at once. "You're giving up."

"Why would you say that?" he shouted back.

"Because you're moving out!" I raised my arms up in exasperation.

"Yeah, to clear my head," he said, now standing in front of me.

We kept arguing, pointing fingers, and blaming one another. We were shouting at each other, completely forgetting that we were not home and this was supposed to be a vacation.

"I'm done!" Alex finally yelled. "I can't keep having this discussion with you over and over again, Gina!"

"No, I'm done, Alex," I said, turned around, and opened the door.

No.

Oh my God, no!

Standing in front of me was Julia. Tears were falling from her eyes, streaking across her sun-kissed cheeks. She was sobbing and visibly shaking.

Alex gasped. I turned to look at him, my eyes pleading for him to find the right words. Instead, he put his hands over his face and fell into the armchair by the window.

I looked at Julia again, my mouth open as I tried to say something, but the words died within me.

There was no more trying to shield our daughters from the truth.

There was no more trying to buy ourselves time before revealing what had happened to our family.

The truth was out.

Our family was officially broken.

Chapter Twelve

"Girls," I said, my arms crossed. "Sit down. Dad has something to tell you."

Julia, Bella, and Olivia joined Alex and me at the kitchen table. Julia had her eyebrow raised and would not stop staring at me. She could sense something big was coming, even though since coming back from Cape Cod a couple of weeks prior, she had not witnessed that many arguments between Alex and me—mainly because Alex was at work the majority of the day.

"What is it?" Bella asked, her leg jittering with impatience and apprehension as she, too, sensed something was off.

"Girls . . ." Alex began, his voice struggling to come out.

From the corner of my eye, I could see that Alex kept glancing at me as if to make sure once more that he had to be the one to reveal the truth to our daughters. I told him multiple times that since this was his mess and his doing, he had to be the one to confess to the girls and tell them he was going to move out. I hoped until the very last moment that he would change his mind about wanting to leave our home, the one we had so happily designed and decorated together. But since coming back from Cape Cod, he had packed a few more clothes every morning.

Having to witness that had slowly chipped away every last hope I had left that we could reconcile or that he would come to his senses and tell me he had changed his mind. But that day never came.

Instead, here we were, sitting around the kitchen table where we had shared so many family meals, conversations about homework, school projects, sports team wins and losses. It was the place where we had teased one another, laughed so hard that food almost came out of our noses, and planned family vacations to create memories that would last us a lifetime. That kitchen table would now be the setting for a conversation I would never have expected us to have.

"There is no easy way to say this, but . . ." Alex broke the silence that had heavily fallen on all of us. He cleared his throat before saying, "your mom and I have decided to separate."

I closed my eyes the moment I heard his voice turning my nightmare into our new reality. I couldn't believe that he had gone through with it. He was actually serious about ending our marriage.

"And I am going to move out," he added in a thin voice.

Bella's sobbing quickly prompted me to open my eyes. She had tears streaming down her face. Olivia was shaking her head no repeatedly and breathing so heavily that I thought she was going to hyperventilate and pass out. Julia had buried her face in her hands, crying in pain.

It was done.

Our family had been destroyed.

I wanted to go and console my girls, but the moment I put weight on my feet to push myself up from the chair, I felt like the room was spinning around me. I grabbed the table to help me stabilize my balance, but my hands did not have enough strength, and I fell back into the chair.

Nobody noticed, though. *God, where are you?*

We were all too busy dealing with the earth-shattering loss of what we knew as family. As I looked around the table, I realized this might have been the last time we sat together in our kitchen. Nothing was ever going to be the way it used to be. Ever again.

Which bank account do we use to pay the bills? I had no idea. Alex had always taken care of our bank accounts, investments, and insurance. How were we going to split them? What was in my name? What was in our joint bank account? I had no clue. Which account did we use for the girls' college funds?

The girls!

That's when I noticed that I had been so lost in my own thoughts that I didn't realize Olivia had left the kitchen, Bella was screaming at Alex because she didn't want him to touch or hug her, and Julia was having a hard time catching her breath because of how hard she was crying.

"Julia," I whispered.

She didn't hear me.

"Julia," I said, this time forcing my tone to be a bit louder in the hope she would hear me.

Her eyes met mine.

"Take a deep breath," I said and took a deep breath as well to try to guide her through regaining control over her breathing.

It didn't work.

"I-I . . ." she muttered, having to force her lips to move and coordinate with her tongue to pronounce the words her heart was screaming. "I wi-wish I weh . . . I wish I were really sick, uh, so Dad wouldn't move out."

I lost it.

Tears began flowing down my cheeks, and I couldn't stop them. My body no longer had the strength to be the adult. I looked at Alex, and even through the veiled and opaque view I had of him from the pools of bitter tears flooding my eyes, I could see his head lowered and lost in his hands.

So you heard it, too, you son of a bitch.

I screamed inside of me.

"You see what you did?" I yelled at him. "This is what you did to your family."

I pointed at Julia, who looked at me as if pleading not to add insult to injury. But I couldn't be the adult at that moment. I couldn't be Mom. I was simply Gina, a woman whose husband had betrayed her. And I was going to let him feel my full wrath.

"Why haven't you told them *the reason* why you want to move out and break us, huh?" I got up, my feet now able to support my weight. I slammed my hands on the wooden table so hard that it shook and added, "You said *we* have decided to separate, but there was no *we* in that decision. I had nothing to do with it. This is all your fault!"

At that point, Bella ran to her room, slamming the door behind her. Olivia did the same. Julia stayed seated and covered her ears with her hands.

Alex looked up, meeting my inflamed gaze. "You want to keep going, or are you done?" he said under his breath, but I heard him loud and clear.

"Are you saying this is my fault?" I screamed, pointing the finger at the empty hallway that both Olivia and Bella had used to run away from the situation and hide in their rooms. "Didn't you hear what I just said? This is all *your* fault! You were the one who destroyed our family, not me. You were the one who wanted to move out, not me. And now you want to turn the tables and blame me for this disaster?"

"Stop it!" Julia yelled before pushing her chair away from the table and running to her bedroom like her sisters.

I sat back down, my arms hanging lifelessly at my sides.

I closed my eyes and took a deep breath.

Alex got up and walked down the hallway, probably to one of their bedrooms. I knew I had to do the same, but I needed a few moments to myself to hopefully regain my composure.

Sitting alone at the table, I looked around the kitchen, which had hosted Olivia's birthday party just the day before. She had turned thirteen years old. We celebrated with all our friends and family as if nothing was wrong. Alex and I did our best not to even look at each other and smiled our most forced smiles for the photos we took.

The kitchen had been the setting for a beautiful occasion, filled with laughter and giggles, with teenagers and grownups singing "Happy Birthday" off-key but in unison, with cheers and best wishes. If I focused on the silence, I could still hear the echo of yesterday's happiness.

A week prior, once again in this very kitchen, we celebrated my birthday. Alex and I pretended to be happy and in love as oblivious family members cheered us on. I barely blew out the candles on my birthday cake. I didn't even try—I had been extremely sick to my stomach the entire day, dreading the show I knew I had to put on later that day.

But I knew that no matter how hard those days had been for me, having to pretend that everything was fine, nothing was going to compare to tomorrow: our anniversary. Just the thought made me want to punch Alex in the face. We had always celebrated our anniversary, and over the years, we had developed a routine: I would choose the restaurant, he would get me flowers, and we would have a romantic dinner.

But he always found ways to surprise me, like the time he bought me a sparkly diamond bracelet from Tiffany—the moment I saw the iconic Tiffany blue case, I felt like Audrey Hepburn in *Breakfast at Tiffany's*—or when he had booked an exotic weekend getaway in the Caribbean just for the two of us. But this year, only one thing awaited us on our special day: the dissolution of our marriage.

I shook my head in an attempt to shoo the thought away, but it didn't work. This was my reality, and I had to come to terms with it. I pushed my palms against the table and forced my legs to carry me to Julia's room. She didn't say anything when I knocked on her door, but her muffled sobs spoke for her.

My firstborn was sprawled across her bed, sobbing into her pillow when I pushed the door open. My fragile heart broke into a million pieces, but I held myself together, sat down next to her, and caressed her hair like when she was a little girl and needed me to do that to fall asleep. I hoped the gesture would help her calm down. It didn't. Instead, it just intensified her wails.

"I'm so sorry," I whispered, biting my lips in an attempt not to start crying again too. Knowing my words couldn't fix the hurt she felt, I kissed her head and walked out of her room.

I made my way to Bella's room but heard Alex's voice before going in.

He must be there with her, I thought.

So I went into Olivia's room, where I found her sitting on her bed, hugging her favorite stuffed animal, her chin buried in it.

"Can I come in?" I asked her while standing on the threshold.

She didn't even look at me, but I could see she had been crying hard because her eyes were red and puffy. But no more tears were coming out.

She must have exhausted them all. That thought made my heart feel even heavier because it meant she was at a point where it hurt so much that she could no longer cry.

"I'm sorry," was all I could say as I crossed the room to her.

Once again, she didn't acknowledge my words.

"Can I sit next to you?" I asked her.

She shook her head no, so I kept standing. I looked around her room and saw frames and frames filled with pictures of happy family memories from all of the fun vacations we had taken together over the years. There was one that especially caught my eye: the five of us posing with big, genuine smiles in front of Cinderella's Castle at the Magic Kingdom in Walt Disney World. We had taken that photo only a few months prior. Yet, it felt like a lifetime ago.

Will we ever have those moments again? I thought. *Will we ever go to Disney World as a family again?* The weight of how uncertain our future was crushed me deep into my soul. Alex had ruined so much. I looked back at Olivia, who was hugging that stuffed animal as if it were a shield. *Her teenage years are going to be marked by her parent's separation,* I suddenly realized.

This thought terrified me: What impact was it going to have on her? With her father being physically gone from our house, was she going to grow up to be one of those girls who looked for a father figure in the first guy she met? Alex had always been a present father, spoiling our daughters but also making sure to parent them and set them up on a path of success and fulfillment. Was he still going to be able to do that once he lived someplace else?

So many questions.

So many doubts.

So many unknowns.

I kissed her forehead and left the room, slowly closing the door behind me. I heard Alex's voice coming from Julia's room, so I went to see how Bella was doing. Judging by her furrowed eyebrows and arms crossed over her chest, I could tell she wanted nothing to do with either Alex or me. I apologized to her, but my words drowned in her painful screams. I didn't kiss her, as she wouldn't let me get close to her.

I felt completely empty. There was nothing else left in me: no energy, no will, perhaps not even a heartbeat. I walked into my bedroom and closed the door behind me, locking it, not caring if Alex couldn't get into the room. I didn't want to be around him. I needed to be alone. I fell on the bed, my head hitting the pillow. My hand pressed against my chest as if the external pressure could stop my heart from breaking apart. So much damage had been done that I no longer had hope for recovery. Nothing was going to be able to patch up this broken heart of mine, nothing.

There was nothing left in me: no energy, no will, and perhaps not even a heartbeat.

I closed my eyes, a single tear leaving its safe harbor to disappear into the cold bedspread, lost forever. I imagined it being me, leaving the life I had known for the past eighteen years, my safe harbor, and forever getting lost in the cold and uncharted territory of a broken family.

I must have fallen asleep that way because, when I woke up, I was on the bedspread rather than under the covers and still in the same clothes I had on the day prior. I squinted as I slowly allowed the sunlight into my life. No alarm had gone off, so I didn't know what time it was. I turned to reach for my phone, but it wasn't on the nightstand. *I must have left it in the kitchen yesterday*, I thought.

I got up, took a shower, and got dressed. But before I opened the door to go to the kitchen, a picture on my bedroom wall caught my eye and took my breath away. It was a photo of Alex and me on our wedding day.

I was in my wedding gown, and Alex was in his tailored suit. We were so young and smiley, our entire life ahead of us, the promise of one day having our own family still intact. I was holding my bouquet proudly, the twinkle in my eye reminding me of how I felt that I was in real life fairytale and had just married my prince charming.

I had passed by that photo every day of my life—we always kept it in our bedroom, even before moving into the new house. I had never noticed it the way I did now, though. I always knew it was there, and sure, I looked at it from time to time, but now it was as if I was seeing it for the first time. I could feel my chest rising higher and higher as my breathing became more labored. My teeth hurt from how hard I was grinding them.

I stared at that younger version of me and wanted to slap her face and wake her up. I stared at the younger version of Alex and wanted to spit in his eyes. I could feel an urge rising within me, and for a moment, I thought about suffocating it and letting it die within me. But that thought left, and I was suddenly free.

Free to let go.

I pulled the photo off the wall and threw it on the bedroom floor.

A guttural scream burst from deep inside me the moment it hit the floor.

Glass shattered everywhere, and I felt a bit lighter. Finally, I no longer had to look at that photo. I turned around and felt haunted. I never realized how many photos of my life with Alex were in our bedroom. I saw one from a cruise we took years prior; I was wearing an evening dress, which I had paired with diamond earrings, while Alex was in a black tuxedo. We were smiling as we posed by the pool outside on the top deck, the night sky sparkling with a million stars that shined brightly thanks to the lack of light pollution.

I smirked.

I took a step closer to it, grabbed it, and threw it on the floor into the never-ending abyss of shattered memories and broken promises.

I felt such a rush of adrenaline when I broke the frame. I loved it. It made me feel like I was finally in control of what was happening around me. I looked for my next victim and found it quickly: Alex's birthday party three years prior. I had planted a big, red-lipped kiss on his cheek as he blew out the candles. I grabbed the photo with both hands, pulled it off the wall, and threw it on the floor.

CRACK!

Broken into a thousand pieces that could never be repaired ever again. I felt out of breath when I saw the ocean of broken glass around me. With my slippers on, I walked all over it, crushing it even more under my feet. I picked up the photo of Alex's birthday and tore it into a million pieces, releasing it into the abyss, scattering it like raindrops over water.

"What are you doing in there?" I heard Alex shout from outside the locked bedroom door.

"Shut up!" I yelled back as I grabbed every frame I could find and smashed it on the floor.

"What are you doing?" he yelled. "Stop it, you're going to wake up the girls, and they're going to be scared!"

His words didn't register.

I kept breaking frames, tearing up photos, and crunching glass.

"Gina!" he shouted.

"I said shut up, you son of a bitch!" I yelled back.

When I was done with the bedroom, I unlocked the door and opened it. Alex was staring at me, his mouth gaping in disbelief at the massacre I had left behind me. I pushed him aside and made my way to the hallway, ready to continue my carnage.

"Mom, no!" Julia yelled behind me when she saw me smash yet another frame.

I didn't reply.

SMASH!

Another frame gone, another picture ripped into a million pieces like the vows Alex had shared with me eighteen years prior before God in church.

"Momma!" Bella screamed between sobs. I turned to look at her, and she was standing by her bedroom door, still in her pajamas. Olivia, whose eyes were puffy and sleepy, ran toward Julia and hid behind her.

Another picture ripped into a million pieces like the vows Alex said to me before God.

"If you girls have something to say, I am not the person to say them to because I didn't cause this," I yelled before throwing one more frame on the floor. "IT'S HIS FAULT!"

I yelled with all my might as I pointed the finger at Alex, who had both hands on his head.

"Gina, stop this," he said without moving.

"I didn't start this," I told him in the calmest tone I could muster.

"Don't you see how much you're scaring the girls?" Alex said.

I could see that, but it was not registering within me. *CRACK!*

"Stop it!" he yelled again. "Why are you doing this?"

I smirked once more and raised my eyebrow to challenge his composure. I knew what I was going to say, but I wanted it to hurt as if he had just been stabbed by all the shattered glass that flooded our home. I opened my arms, looked around, and in a singsong tone, said, "Celebrating our anniversary."

PART THREE
How to Trust God

Chapter Thirteen

"**M**om, don't cry," Olivia whispered while sitting on my bed next to me and caressing my shoulder.

"I'm sorry you have to see me like this," I said as I covered my face with my hands.

After months and months of arguing, Alex had officially moved out, and he had just left with the last of his belongings. His side of the closet was now empty, as was the space he used to occupy in our bed. Knowing that this was no longer *our* home, the one where we would grow old as husband and wife, brought such heaviness to my chest that it made it hard for me to take deep, cleansing breaths.

But I knew I didn't want to let my emotions get the best of me as I did on our eighteenth wedding anniversary. That was certainly not my proudest moment. I saw how much my uncontrolled behavior had scared the girls, and I promised myself I would never allow it to happen ever again.

"I told you that you should have gone to the concert with Julia and Bella," I said to Olivia, forcing a smile as I dried my tears with my open palm.

"Yeah, well," she said with a shrug. "I didn't want to go. I wanted to stay with you."

I looked into Olivia's eyes and felt my heart skip a beat. At her age, I spent my free time roller skating, not consoling my mother or trying to figure out life with separated parents. She had just entered her adolescence, and this was certainly not a great way to get started.

"Well," I said, shaking my head, "it's getting late, and I don't feel like cooking."

"Mom," Olivia said, one eyebrow raised to tease me. "You never feel like cooking."

We both giggled. The sensation felt foreign, but it was welcomed.

"True," I admitted. "But tonight, I *really* don't feel like cooking. What do you say we order pizza?"

"Yay!" Olivia cheered.

"Alright, I'll go to the kitchen to order." I said. "I left my phone there."

"Can I choose a movie to watch?" Olivia asked.

"Of course," I said, caressing her cheek.

I was not in the mood to eat or watch TV, but I wanted to distract Olivia from the chaos I had inside of me. After ordering pizza, I retired to my room to do some breathing exercises, though I found it hard to focus because my mind was spinning out of control in a What If game.

What if Alex never comes back to me?

What if being a single mother is really my life now?

What if my daughters never recover from this shock?

What if God doesn't answer my prayers?

I grabbed my hair as if it might help get rid of these toxic thoughts that were haunting my mind and terrifying my heart.

"Mom, the pizza delivery guy is here," Olivia called from the hallway.

"Be right there," I yelled.

As I passed in front of the mirror on my way out, I glanced at my reflection. Judging by the dark circles around my eyes, I could tell my body was suffering from the consequences of my emotional distress. I knew I had to get my emotions under control because they had been spilling everywhere, tainting whatever they came in contact with.

I took a deep breath and told myself, "This will get easier." The thought that perhaps the worst was behind me brought a sense of weightlessness inside me as my heart felt momentarily free from burden and pain. I sighed and joined my daughter for dinner.

But things did not get easier.

As days turned into weeks and weeks turned into months, I found myself facing one crisis after another, and it seemed that all Alex and I could do was argue.

It all started when, one day, he sent me a message that read: "I have to tell you something."

Oh no, I thought as I hunched over, holding onto my stomach that was instantly in pain.

I was sitting on the couch in the living room, where I had been writing in my journal—something I started doing the moment he moved out. I put my journal on the end table next to me and waited for the next message. But I could sense he was about to reveal something I certainly did not want to hear. Female intuition, perhaps.

"I have had multiple affairs since Julia was born."

Multiple affairs.

Multiple affairs.
Multiple affairs.

I read that segment over and over to make sure my brain was actually processing the exact words he had written and was not making anything up.

My brain had not been making anything up. Those were the words Alex had written.

Julia was sixteen years old.

He's been having affairs for sixteen years.

We had been married for eighteen years, and for sixteen of those years, he had been having affairs?

My entire marriage was a lie.

I threw my phone across the room but felt my breathing become more and more labored. As my eyes closed and I leaned back against the couch, a tingling sensation spread throughout my body, making it feel numb. I knew what was happening: I was having another panic attack.

Panic attacks had happened frequently since our trip to Mexico, and I was now able to recognize them quickly and knew how to calm myself down. First, I took off my slippers and put my warm feet on the cold floor. The difference in temperature sent a shockwave up my spine that helped me ground myself in the moment. As my heavy breathing came under control, I placed one hand over my heart and the other on my stomach and engaged in breathing exercises.

When I felt the attack lessen, I stood up, picked up my phone from the floor, and stared at it. I wanted to call Alex and scream at him. But that wouldn't have gotten me anywhere. It would have only worked me up even more and perhaps even brought on another panic attack. I needed to send Alex a clear message on how I felt about what he did to me, to us. But my words wouldn't suffice. I needed action, something that proved to him I could unravel his life, too. So, I called my cousin, who was a lawyer.

"Hey," I said after she picked up. "I want to divorce Alex."

"What?" she asked, more out of shock than anything else. She was aware of Alex's betrayal—as were all of our family members and friends by now—but I could tell by her high-pitched tone that she was not expecting to hear these words come out of my mouth.

"I want to divorce Alex," I said again to let her know I was serious and firm in my decision. "And you have to help me."

"But Gina—"

"I want to divorce Alex," I said, interrupting her, this time my tone higher to convey just how determined I was.

She sighed heavily. I couldn't see her, but I would bet that she was shaking her head no in resignation.

"Alright," she said. "Let's meet soon to discuss the terms of the divorce."

"I'm free tomorrow," I said. "I'll stop by your office in the morning."

Immediately after hanging up the phone, my fingers flew furiously across the keyboard. "I've hired a lawyer," I texted Alex. "You will be served with divorce papers soon." My gloves had come off, and I vowed to myself never to put them back on.

Our separation—soon to be divorce—had turned ugly rather quickly, especially because Alex had taken his gloves off as well. Not only had he moved out, but he was also still seeing her.

My friends Maureen and Monica—who completely missed their life calling as private investigators—would often text me photos they had secretly snapped of them whenever they saw them out together. Every time I received a photo, I felt the urge to punch him in the face and give him a piece of my mind. It seemed that every two weeks, something—a new photo or a new revelation—would come up; we would settle one argument and then start the next. Over and over again, it felt like I was going around in a vicious cycle of toxicity. I couldn't take it anymore. I wanted out of that painful vortex but couldn't because I wasn't the one who had created it in the first place.

I wanted out of that painful vortex.

One day, after seeing the umpteenth photo of Alex and her together, I just fell on my bedroom floor, surrounded by the shadows of my betrayal. I curled into the fetal position, my hands holding onto my knees, bent enough to touch my chin. Tears gathered on the floor in a pool of desperation and hopelessness.

"Gina!" I heard a familiar voice say, but my eyes were closed. I didn't want to see the emptiness of my reality.

"Oh my God . . ." she said, as I felt her hand move my hair away from my eyes. "I must have called you a thousand times and got so worried when you didn't pick up. Now I know why. Come on, let me help you up."

Gwen held my hand in an attempt to help me stand up. I whimpered. She couldn't do it that way; I was dead weight. She walked around me, placed her hands underneath my armpits, and slowly succeeded in pulling me up. She helped me get on my bed. My desperation had reached a new level of scary. But what truly terrified me and kept me up at night was knowing this was not the end.

A few days later, Alex told me he had rented a house five houses down the hill from where the girls and I lived. He said he had rented that house to be close to the girls to make sure he wouldn't miss out on anything.

My response was, "If you really cared about being close to the girls, you would have never betrayed me or destroyed our family."

Alex didn't like it when I threw the truth in his face, but that's how we kept going at each other, trying to hurt each other more than we were being hurt. Our conversations escalated fast into full-blown arguments that left me feeling completely void of emotions and energy.

I often felt as though I was walking around with only half of my heart. No one asked me how my day was or cared if I was home. I no longer belonged to anyone. I was alone, floating out in the world.

The only things that helped me move forward during this difficult time were going to church regularly, reading the Bible I kept in my nightstand, and writing in my journal. I felt that church allowed me to understand my place in the world, and the reassurance that God's love was everlasting brought me comfort and hope. Writing gave me a chance to vent without speaking. Releasing my uncensored thoughts and feelings onto paper was truly therapeutic; once those emotions were on the page, they were no longer in my heart.

Church allowed me to understand my place in the world, and the reassurance that God's love was everlasting brought me comfort and hope.

Meanwhile, I did my best not to get our daughters hurt in the crossfire. Unfortunately, I was not always able to protect them. One evening, I was on the phone with my sister and venting about my broken marriage.

"I feel that perhaps I could have forgiven his one affair, you know," I said as I could feel tears gathering in my eyes. "I could have forgiven him if he was truly repentant. We all make mistakes, and maybe we could have moved on from that betrayal. But the fact that he's been having affairs on and off since Julia was born is what really kills me," I managed to say before my tears took over, and I started sobbing on the phone.

I was so caught up in my conversation and emotions that I did not notice my bedroom door was ajar. Before I knew it, I heard footsteps stomping down the hallway and loud sighs.

"Oh no," I said to my sister. "I think the girls overheard what I just told you. I gotta go."

After tossing my phone on the bed (I hoped I'd hung up), I dashed to my door and looked outside. Bella and Olivia were standing there, shaking, unable to even cry.

"I'm so sorry," I said as I walked toward them to hug them, but they took a step back, refusing the comfort of my arms.

I looked up and saw that Julia's bedroom door was wide open, her light on. *She must have been the one running down the hallway*, I thought.

"Julia?" I called, but she didn't answer. I could hear her cry, her sobs muffled by what I assumed was her pillow.

Alex had never explained to the girls why we had decided to separate, and I hated that this was how they found out. But, unfortunately, I knew that sooner or later, they would have learned the truth one way or another. I just didn't want them to hear it coming from me.

"Is that true, Mom?" Bella asked, still shaking as if she were cold.

I looked at her, caressed her hair, and nodded yes.

"Mom . . ." Olivia said as she burst out in tears and hid her face on my shoulder. I hugged her tight, wishing I could take all that pain away from her forever.

"I don't want to spend Christmas with Dad," Julia said after she stepped out of her room, her hair in disarray and eyes red with the bitter tears of betrayal.

"Well, we decided that you were going to spend Christmas here at the house and then go to Dad's on Christmas night, remember?" I said, hoping she had just forgotten and that she'd be fine with spending Christmas night with her dad—though I couldn't help but feel a bit relieved knowing the girls wanted to stay with me.

"I remember," she said as she crossed her arms. "But I am not going."

I opened my mouth to try to remind her that he was still her dad and that he would be heartbroken if she didn't want to go and spend the day with him, but Bella stopped me before any words could come out.

"Me neither!" Bella said, stepping toward Julia.

"I'm not going to his house ever again," Olivia said, drying her tears with the corner of her shirt and joining her older sisters.

It was three against one. My heart was torn. What was I supposed to do? Part of me wanted to insist on having them spend the day with their father. He had always been present in their lives, and regardless of how much he worked, he always made it a point to spend one-on-one time with each of them—not to mention, I knew Alex was going to be devastated if they didn't go. Part of me, however, wanted to respect the way they felt about the situation and give them the time they needed to process what they had just learned.

I looked at them, standing close to each other, their lips thin with anger and resentment as they stared back at me. I realized this was a pivotal moment in this big shift in family dynamics we were all going through.

This was the moment that was going to decide who our daughters could count on. Yes, Alex was going to be sad that the girls didn't want to spend time with him, but wasn't that just one of the many consequences of his actions? He was an adult and would have to deal with what he had coming.

"Alright," I said, slowly walking toward the girls and opening my arms to invite them all into a Mama Bear hug. "Let's not decide anything now, okay?"

The three of them hinted at a smile and melted in my arms. I closed my eyes and squeezed them tight. At that moment, I realized that being a single mother meant that, more often than not, I was going to have to tend to the scars their father had caused. While I couldn't make them go away, I could at least alleviate the pain, and that meant a lot to me.

The next morning, as expected, Alex did not take the news well. He accused me of pitting them against him, manipulating them into thinking he was a monster, and letting them know about his affairs on purpose.

I listened to his accusations and knew I couldn't react because the girls needed me to be strong. I was so tired of this back-and-forth with him and all the bickering that had been going on for months. It kept me up at night, and, as a result of not getting rest, I felt tired and on edge during the day. This had to stop.

"Alex," I said. "I can't keep going like this, with the two of us always arguing."

He sighed.

"The holidays are going to be hard for all of us because this is going to be the first Christmas we spend as a . . ." I paused as the words were getting lost in the lump I felt in my throat. I took a deep breath and said, "broken family. There will be many other occasions where we won't be spending time together for the first time, and we just have to do the best we can without adding unnecessary and painful arguments to the mix."

"Like the yearly trip to Disney World in February," Alex added, almost in a whisper.

"Yes," I said.

"Can I come to that one at least, please?" Alex asked. I could hear the pain in his voice. Yes, he was the one who had caused this whole implosion, but that didn't mean he wasn't suffering, too.

Is he starting to realize just how much he gave up?

"I don't know, Alex," I said. "I'll have to think about it."

"Okay," he said. "I understand."

We hung up, and I went to take a much-needed warm bath, though I was having a hard time relaxing because I kept thinking of Alex wanting to come to Disney. The theme parks had always been such a precious location to us, a place where we could escape from it all and truly spend quality time together as a family. Every year, Alex and I felt as though our relationship grew stronger after spending time at Disney World. There was just something about that magical place that brought us closer together. Would the magic work again?

Perhaps he should come, I thought. *It might be the only way for us to get back what we once had.*

But I knew he was still seeing her sporadically, so there was no way I would want to go on such a special family vacation with him. That is unless I knew Alex had ended it with her and wanted to focus back on us, on rebuilding our relationship.

Yes, I can make that stipulation, I thought.

✝

And I did. Once the holiday season was over and February was approaching, I wrote Alex a letter explaining that if he wanted to come to Disney with us, it had to be because he wanted to work on us. He fought my stipulation, and we got into yet another argument, which ultimately ended in him saying he would not be joining the yearly family vacation.

My stomach flipped upside down for how frustrated I was with him, the situation, and knowing I couldn't possibly go to Disney with just the girls. That place held way too many memories of Alex and me as a married couple—as a *happily* married couple—and I couldn't handle going there without him. It would have tainted the magic forever for me.

Still, I wanted the girls to have their yearly trip to the sunshine state—a great way for us to leave the cold Upstate New York weather for a few days—so I booked us amazing suites at the Ritz-Carlton in Naples, Florida. Just scrolling through the resort's website put me in a good mood: images of breathtaking sunsets, fun pool slides that I knew the girls were going to love, and an overall relaxed and inviting atmosphere.

Just what I need, I thought as I smiled. I knew we were going to have a good time there, far away from all the bitterness and senseless bickering. Though, if I had to be honest, I couldn't help but hope that Alex would fly down to surprise us.

But the surprise never came. The shock, however, did. While the girls and I were enjoying being with our toes in the warm sand and taking photos by the sea, I found out—through pictures from my friend Stacy—that Alex had decided to spend those same days with her.

Now he is taking her to a family gathering? I thought. I couldn't believe it. One moment I was admiring the sunset on the Gulf from the private balcony of my room, and the next, I was in a bottomless pit of despair.

This is it.

I'm done with him.

I decided that when I got back to New York, I was going to push the express button on my divorce. He needed a clear signal from me that his behavior was unacceptable, and even though my cousin and I had been putting off talks on how to proceed with the papers and the filing, I now knew what I had to do—I was going to get it done once and for all.

There was no more hope of reconciliation for Alex and me.

I just needed to accept it and move on with my life.

The last few days of our vacation were a blur. I was physically there, but mentally I was someplace else. I was in a world of my own, made of divorce papers, what-ifs, and many questions about my future. The girls noticed, of course, but they didn't force me to tell them what was going on. I guess they knew they would find out eventually.

Once back in New York, I immediately got a hold of my cousin and told her I wanted to meet with her to move forward with the filing.

"Are you sure?" she asked. "It's been over seven months since you first said you were going to move forward with it."

"This time, I mean it," I told her.

I looked at myself in the mirror before going to the car, and what I saw made me question who in the world I had become. I had not been eating well, wasn't working out, and I hadn't been sleeping or resting. I sighed and shook my head. *This nightmare needs to be over.*

This nightmare needs to be over.

As I waited at a stoplight for the light to change, I felt an itch on my breast. I went to scratch it and—

A lump.

My heart jumped in my throat.

A lump.

I touched it, pressed it, and felt it around.

I have a lump in my breast.

I froze.

This can't be happening. *Oh, God. Please. I can't handle one more thing.*

Okay, don't panic, I tried to reassure myself. *This is new, yes, but it doesn't mean it's cancer.*

My heart was beating so fast that I felt the vein in my neck pulsating.

I had a mammogram two years ago, and they didn't find anything, so it's probably nothing because breast cancer doesn't develop this quickly, does it?

BEEP! BEEP!

The cars behind me honked, and I jumped out of my skin with fear. I looked at the stoplight and noticed it was green—and judging by how empty the lane next to mine was and how far away the cars in front of me were, it was clear it had been green for a while. I raised my right hand to apologize to those who had been waiting on me and drove straight back home.

I ran to the bathroom, took my shirt off, and checked myself in the mirror. I touched the lump over and over again, trying to make sense of what was happening to me.

It's still here.

I picked up the phone and called my gynecologist. Thankfully, he was able to see me that same day, so I drove myself to her office. I was shaking and shivering with fear when I called my sister—who didn't live close by—and explained what had happened.

It felt like time had slowed down and sped up all at the same time. I couldn't think straight. My cousin had messaged me multiple times, asking me if I was still going to meet with her. I read her messages, but they didn't make sense to me. Nothing mattered at that moment. I had a lump in my breast, and that was the only thing I could think of.

In the doctor's office, my doctor had me take my shirt and bra off and asked me to lie down. Seconds turned into hours as I was examined. "Yes," he whispered as he touched the area where I had felt the lump. "I feel it too."

I gasped.

I had hoped he would tell me I had imagined everything. Instead, there it was.

"But don't worry," he said, probably sensing the desperation I had just fallen into. "I don't think this is anything to worry about. But, out of an abundance of caution, I'd say you need to go get a mammogram."

He wrote me a referral to a screening center, and I scheduled the appointment right away for the next morning. Once there, I slowly walked toward the entrance, though I couldn't feel my body move. It was as if my legs were robotically carrying the rest of my body, which felt numb and detached from the rest of the world.

Inside the reception, the atmosphere was cold: white, sterile walls framed the sense of despair and unknown that engulfed me. The condescending tone of the receptionist was a sharp razor slowly slithering through my already broken soul as she reassured me that the technician would call me soon for the mammogram.

I sat next to an end table adorned with a pile of fitness and gossip magazines. Smiling women with a seemingly carefree attitude on every cover seemed to mock me, and I felt the urge to throw them across the room. I bit my bottom lip, looked up toward the hall, and saw a man wearing a green lab coat walk toward me. Since I was the only patient in the waiting room, I knew he was coming for me.

I held my breath.

"Mrs. Tronco?" he asked with a smile.

No, I thought. *I am about to be a divorced woman. Mrs. Tronco will soon be no more.*

I nodded yes.

"Hello, my name is . . ."

I couldn't follow what he was saying. I tried reading his lips, but my brain wasn't connecting. So, my robotic legs carried me down the hall and into the room he had previously emerged from.

Once the mammogram was done, I put my clothes back on and was about to walk out of the room when—

"Ma'am," the technician said. "The doctor would like to talk to you, so please wait for him before you go back home."

This can't be a good sign . . .

My legs were jittering, and I was extremely cold, even though it was a warm, sunny day outside. Somehow, I managed to make it to a chair far away from the magazines to wait.

"Mrs. Tronco," the nurse called. "The doctor will see you now."

I got up and followed the nurse to the exam room.

She invited me to sit down and told me the doctor would be in shortly.

I looked around the room and saw posters that tried to put a positive spin on breast cancer: "Early detection can save your life," one poster read under a photo of a smiling woman. "Metastatic breast cancer?" the other read with a logo of some pharmaceutical company. My elbows fell on my knees, and I hid my face in my hands.

"Hello," the doctor greeted me as he entered the room. "How are you?"

"I've been better," I said with a thin voice. My mouth was extremely dry, so much so that it was hard to move my tongue. "So, what's going on?" I needed to cut to the chase. I had no energy for small talk.

"Mrs. Tronco," the doctor said, his tone somber. "Your mammogram shows a lump, and just to rule anything out, we recommend getting a biopsy."

God, please help me.

I nodded to acknowledge I had heard him, but words failed me.

God, please help me.

"You have to be here tomorrow morning at 8 a.m.," he said softly.

I nodded yes.

God, give me strength.

He scheduled the biopsy for the next day, and I slowly walked out of the room. When I called my sister, I broke down in tears. Her words held me up and helped me walk to my car. She stayed on the phone with me the entire drive home. On the way, she suggested I call Alex to tell him I needed to talk to him in person about something important. I had no energy to think of whether or not that was a good idea. So, I followed her suggestion and did what she said.

Alex came to see me at the house ten minutes after I had gotten back home. I didn't want to talk to him, but I knew I had to explain what was happening to me. We sat down at the kitchen table, and after I was done, we both cried.

"I don't want the girls to know anything," I managed to say. "Not until I know what's actually going on."

"Okay," he said. "I won't tell them."

That night, I didn't get any sleep. I stared at the ceiling the entire time, touching the lump in my breast from time to time, each time hoping it had somehow disappeared and this nightmare could finally end. I turned my head to look at the space that Alex used to occupy. His side of the bed was still neatly made, and his pillow was empty. I longed to be held by him. I longed for him to tell me everything was going to be okay. I longed for him to tell me he was going to protect me. But silence and emptiness filled the room.

I was alone.

I cried.

I prayed.

The next morning after I got the girls to school, I went in for the biopsy. Alone. My sister lived two hours away, and I was adamant that I was going alone and didn't need anyone with me—and I sure as hell didn't want Alex with me.

The biopsy was terribly painful, and I cried throughout the procedure, but I did my best not to complain because I just wanted it to be done and over with.

"We'll call you when we have the results," the nurse told me before I left the clinic.

I drove back home, but I couldn't remember the drive. I prepared dinner that night for the girls, but I couldn't remember actually making anything. I went grocery shopping the next day, but I didn't remember ever being in the supermarket. All I could do was check my phone every few seconds.

When are they going to call? I kept thinking.

I just wanted to know. Good or bad, I wanted to know because the wait was killing me.

More hours went by, and still no news. I had called the hospital multiple times to make sure they had not called me—they hadn't—and to see if they had received the results yet.

"Not yet," was the reply I always got from the physician's assistant. "Don't worry. We'll call you when we have the results back."

That sentence was starting to sound like an empty promise.

A day went by, and no news from the doctor.

Then, as I was driving back home from dropping the girls off at school, my phone rang.

I couldn't see the number, so I answered it via Bluetooth. "Hello?"

"Hello, is it Gina Tronco?" an unfamiliar voice asked.

"This is she," I said.

"Gina, this is Mary at the hospital."

Oh my God.

This was it. This was the call.

"We have the results back from the biopsy. Where are you?" she said in a soft voice.

"Ehm . . ." I looked around to see where I was. I couldn't figure it out, even though I had been doing this same drive for years. "I'm in the car."

"Are you driving?" she asked.

"Yes," I said, feeling my tears choking me.

"Gina," she said, her tone even softer now. "Would you please pull over?"

"Okay." I bit my bottom lip to try to hold back tears.

"Just let me know when you've pulled over."

"I have," I said. My heart felt like it was about to leap out of my chest. My hands were shaking so much I couldn't hold the steering wheel. My legs felt completely numb to the point I could no longer feel the pedals under my feet.

"Gina," she said but paused to take a deep breath, which I heard over the phone.

God, please hold my hand.

I closed my eyes.

I held my breath.

I braced for impact.

Then I heard her pronounce the words I'd feared since I found the lump: "You have breast cancer."

Chapter Fourteen

"I have cancer," I said all in one breath as soon as Alex picked up his phone. I knew he was at work, but I didn't care. I knew I was still parked on the side of the road, but I didn't care. My life as I had known it up until that point had ended the moment the doctor gave me the news. I needed Alex now more than ever.

"Oh my God . . ." was all he had the strength to say before he broke down in tears and painful sobs.

I have cancer. I, too, began crying because the moment I heard my own voice pronounce those words, it suddenly became even more real.

I have cancer.

My entire body was shaking so violently that the phone fell out of my hand. My eyes were so full of tears that my vision was blurred, and I couldn't see where it had fallen, so I began blindly touching around my seat when I finally felt it under the palm of my hand. I picked it back up and heard Alex taking deep breaths.

"What did the doctor say?" Alex asked in a thin voice. "What type of cancer is it?"

"She said something about estrogen positive, progesterone positive, HER2-negative, and staged at 2, I think," I said, somewhat matter-of-factly, as if repeating something I had memorized but not comprehended.

"What does it mean?" Alex asked. "Is it bad?"

"I don't know," I confessed. "I'll have to ask when I see the doctor, I guess."

"Alright," he said. "This is what we are going to do. I will call an oncologist so you can be seen right away, okay?"

I nodded, though Alex couldn't see me. Then I grabbed a tissue from my purse and blew my nose.

"Meanwhile, you should go tell your parents," he said.

Oh no!

My parents, who were still heartbroken over my separation from Alex, had no idea I had even gotten a mammogram. I hadn't told them because I kept thinking that it was not going to be anything to worry about, so why alert them? Now I had to tell them that not only had I gotten a mammogram, but that I also got a biopsy, and it turned out it was breast cancer.

"Okay," I whispered.

I knew I had no choice. This had to be done—and quickly too. Better rip the Band-Aid off all at once.

"Be careful when driving," Alex said, knowing I was in no condition to drive because of my mental state but also knowing I had no other option.

I was alone in the car, and nobody could come to my rescue. *God, please tell me why this is happening. Please tell me You can handle this too.* After my silent prayer, I took a deep breath, told Alex I'd talk to him later, and drove to the deli. When I arrived, I had trouble finding a parking spot because the parking lot was packed with cars from the many customers. I did the best I could with the little parking space left, turned the car off, and walked inside.

As I excused my way through the many people waiting in line, I heard my mom say, "Well, this is a surprise!" With a big smile on her face, she waved at me the moment our eyes met. But that was also when her smile quickly straightened into thin lips as she recognized that the expression on my face couldn't translate into good news.

I walked up to her and, in the chaos of the chatter from customers who were busy with their shopping and orders, I said, "Mom, can we go in the back kitchen? I have something to tell you."

I couldn't ask my dad to come, too, because he had to stay and help the customers.

My mom followed me into the kitchen. I walked closer to her and, in one breath, said, "I have breast cancer."

"What?" my dad said, startling me by suddenly popping up behind me.

I turned and saw his face was completely pale, as if the life had just been drained out of him. Now standing between my mom and dad, I felt compelled to bring them up to speed as quickly as possible on what had been going on with me in the past few days.

"I found a lump in my right breast and got a mammogram, which confirmed I had one," I began. "Then the biopsy revealed it's cancer. I have cancer." Tears rushed down my cheeks once again.

My mom and dad stepped closer to me, but they were lost for words. Instead, a veil of dread and worry covered their faces. I went on to explain that Alex was taking care of the next steps and that I didn't want the girls to know about any of this for now. "Tomorrow night, Julia has her prom, and I don't want anything to ruin that experience for her. The girls have already gone through so much these past eight months. I need them to be kids for a few more days before they become the children whose mother is fighting against breast cancer."

All my parents had the strength to do was nod, cry, and pace around in disbelief. Feeling awful, I told them I needed to go back home because I had a busy afternoon with all the prom-related preparations and last-minute arrangements.

I kissed them both goodbye and turned to leave, feeling like the worst daughter ever because, once again, I had dropped a huge bombshell on them. And now they had to somehow get through the day, with the deli even more crowded with people and orders than when I first walked in.

Once I was back in my car, I grabbed my phone from my purse and called my sister. After explaining everything that happened after the biopsy, she said, "Alright, we need to get a team of naturopathic doctors. We have to start fighting this cancer from every angle!"

I sighed.

"Did you tell Mom and Dad?" she asked.

"I just did," I said. "I'm actually still in the parking lot at the deli."

"Well, you sure have some timing," she said. "I'll bet it was packed in there with the lunch crowd. You do choose your moments, huh?"

I couldn't help but smile the faintest smile and shake my head. Of course, how could I not think this was not the best time to tell such devastating news to my parents? The deli was filled with people.

My sister was right; I sure chose my moments. I shook my head and said, "Gosh, I know, but I can't think straight."

"I can tell," my sister said. Then she took a deep breath and added, "Listen to me."

At those words, I sat up straight.

"This is not meant to be something you can't face," she paused briefly to ensure her words had time to sink in. "This is here to teach a lesson. You are meant to learn something truly important from this."

This is here to teach a lesson. I sighed.

My sister, being a firm believer in a holistic approach, clean eating, and energy healing, always found a way to make me see things from her point of view, which I found reassuring and hopeful.

"It is the right breast, correct?" she asked.

"Yeah," I said in a small voice, looking down.

"The right side is hurt because of a refusal to nourish yourself," she said. "And you basically just lost twenty pounds, so there's that. Also, this is where you store anger and resentment, which is something you've been doing for a while. And last but not least: the right side is a male wound connection. This cancer is meant to teach you that you have to fix something in your life that has to do with love and relationships."

Well, that couldn't have been clearer.

I wanted to believe her. I needed to believe her. This cancer was not here to bring even more devastation to my life but to bring me out of the devastation surrounding me. But that required an amount of strength I wasn't sure I had at that very moment. I wanted to fight, but I felt as though I needed a moment to absorb what was happening around me and to me before I could put my boxing gloves on and kick cancer's ass.

Beep beep.

"Oh," I said, looking at my phone. "Alex is calling me, sorry. I have to pick up."

"No worries," my sister said. "Remember what I said and call me when you have news. I want to come with you to your doctor's appointments, okay?"

"Okay," I said. "Will do."

I hung up with her and picked up Alex's call.

"Hey," Alex said, sounding somewhat out of breath. "So, ugh, this is so ridiculous because all these doctors are making me go round and round."

"What's going on?" I asked.

"Well, I called an oncology office, but they said you need to have the CT scan done first. So I called the hospital to schedule it, but they said you have to see a radiologist first. I called the radiologist, and they said you have to see your primary doctor first," Alex said. "This is a huge mess."

"I'm so sorry this is so complicated," I said.

"Not your fault," he said, his tone sounding reassuring. "There's gotta be a faster and easier way to sort this out. Just don't worry about it for now. I'll take care of it."

"Thank you so much," I said, feeling as though that huge weight on my chest that had been preventing me from breathing had momentarily been lifted.

"What time is your spa appointment today with Julia?" Alex asked.

"Oh!" I had totally forgotten about the spa appointment I had booked to pamper my girl before prom. "It's in two hours. Why?"

"Just wanted to know. I couldn't remember. Just try to relax and enjoy your girl time, okay?" Alex was calm and reassuring. It reminded me of the man I used to think my husband was.

"I'll do my best," I said.

After the call ended, I realized that we had just had the first conversation in a long time that didn't involve mentions of divorce, lawyers, affairs, and so on. It felt good. I knew we were not together, but that was the most normal conversation we had had in a long time, one of those conversations we had when we were still happily married. I knew I wasn't supposed to make a mountain out of a molehill, but life had smacked me so hard in the face that day that I decided I deserved to hang on to whatever lifeline I could find.

And at that moment, the conversation with Alex was my lifeline because, regardless of what had been going on between us, the fact that he was doing all he could to help proved to me that his love for me was still there, whether he wanted to admit it or not.

†

The afternoon went by in a blur. I tried my best to enjoy my time with Julia at the spa, but I often caught myself wandering off and getting lost in the what-ifs while we were getting our manicures and pedicures. The same happened when Alex, the girls, and I took prom photos at the country club. I had to force myself to smile during our family photos for two reasons: we were no longer a family, and I was keeping yet one more secret from my girls.

That evening, Alex came by the house to see me. He smiled at me when he saw me, something he hadn't done in a really long time. That smile brought me a hint of hope, but it also reminded me of what I had lost. All I wanted to do was to forget about everything that was happening and go back eight months. I wanted to still be happily married to him. I wanted to be planning our next vacation.

I wanted to be sitting around the kitchen table with my family and having them complain I couldn't cook anything but chicken.

"I'm going to take the girls to my house tonight," he said. "And I'll text Julia and tell her to just drive to my house after prom."

His smile brought me a hint of hope, but it also reminded me of what I had lost.

"Why?" I asked.

"Because I want you to have the night to yourself," he said.

I was going to tell Alex I didn't feel like being alone, but before I could, he took me by the hand and invited me to sit on the couch with him. I sat up straight as he scootched closer to me and looked me deep in the eyes. "Listen, I can't even begin to imagine what you are going through. But I know it's important for you to let your emotions out. I want you to take tonight to let it all out, okay?"

I nodded as I felt tears already rushing to my eyes.

"But hey," Alex leaned in closer. "You only get this one night, you hear me? I won't allow you to feel sorry for yourself after tonight. This is not how we are going to face this situation. No, you are going to go on Amazon tonight and buy yourself a Wonder Woman cape."

I laughed.

"I'm not joking," he said, staring into my eyes and still holding my hand. "You are going to buy yourself that cape, and you are going to hang it in our—" he caught himself and cleared his voice. "—your bedroom where you can constantly see it. I want it to remind you that you are a fighter, a warrior. This is not going to break you. Got it?"

I nodded.

"Good," he said, suddenly letting go of my hand as if he remembered we were no longer together. I didn't force the issue. I simply enjoyed the natural beauty of the moment.

Alex left the room to help the girls get their overnight bags ready and then came back to the couch, where I was still sitting.

"Okay, we're off," he said. "Enjoy your evening."

"I will," I said and then kissed the girls goodnight before they walked out of the door with Alex.

The house was suddenly empty.

I slowly walked around the kitchen, the living room, and down the hall toward the bedrooms. Each bedroom door was slightly open to reveal the void inside. No laughter, no arguments, no music. Nothing. That emptiness, that silence, that void were too much to handle for me.

I walked into my bedroom and closed the door behind me. Emotion escaped from every cell of my body as I collapsed onto the bed. Tears rushed down my cheeks so violently that I felt like they were burning my skin. I cried hard and loud and then crawled to my pillow. As I sobbed, I pulled my legs to my chest and buried my face and desperation in my knees. I cried so much that my body was shaking with pain and torment. The what-ifs were haunting my mind, scaring me to my very core.

What if I won't be there to see my girls graduate?

Tears rushed from my eyes.

What if I won't be there to help my girls choose a wedding gown?

I hugged my legs even tighter.

What if I won't be there to hold my first grandchild?

I couldn't breathe.

"God," I said between sobs. "Please help me . . . I don't understand why all of this is happening to me."

I reached for my Bible on my nightstand. My tears staining the cover, I said, "Please, God, I am terrified."

I opened the Bible and scrolled through the pages until a quote I wrote on a page caught my attention. Through sobs, I read: "God won't give you more than HE can handle."

God won't give you more than HE can handle.

I read that quote over and over.

Suddenly, my shoulders felt warm, as if a loving embrace had just blanketed them.

I read that quote again.

My sobs quieted down.

I caressed the quote with my trembling finger and took a deep breath.

Bzzt.

My phone vibrated. I turned to look at my nightstand, where my phone was. I sat the Bible next to me on the bed and grabbed the phone. A message from Alex. I clicked on it and read: "Buy the cape."

I smiled and wiped my eyes with my sleeve.

I went on Amazon, looked for the Wonder Woman cape, and when I found it, I clicked on *Buy Now*.

Then, I went back to Alex's message and replied: "I just did."

That night, I wrote in my journal, read the Bible quote a few more times, and fell asleep with a heart filled with hope. After all, I had just bought myself a Wonder Woman cape.

Chapter Fifteen

"**G**irls, it's going to be okay," I said with a smile in the most reassuring voice I could possibly muster.

Alex, the girls, and I were sitting around the table in the kitchen, which by now had become the official Situation Room of the Tronco household, where all the most sensitive issues that afflicted our family were discussed. Only eight months prior, we were sitting in this very room when Alex told the girls about our separation.

The guilt I felt in telling the girls about my cancer diagnosis weighed heavily on my chest as if it were a ton of bricks. But now it was done.

While my approach to the diagnosis reveal was different from the separation reveal—mainly because I didn't want the girls to worry, so I acted like it wasn't that big of a deal—the girls took it just as bad, with Bella sobbing so hard that her tears were cascading down her face uncontrollably, Olivia shaking her head no repeatedly, and Julia crying away in pain while coming over to hug me. Then, just as it happened last time, all three of them stood up and ran to their respective bedrooms, shutting their doors behind them.

I was going to go see them one at a time and hug them tight like only a mother can. But first, I needed a moment to gather my energy.

Now alone with Alex, I leaned back into the chair as my arms fell to the sides. I looked up at the ceiling and prayed silently.

God, please give strength to Julia, Bella, and Liv. They need you to guide them through this ordeal as much as I do.

"I called the concierge doctor in Boston," Alex said, calling my attention.

The day prior, my mom had called me to let me know that she had spoken with one of the regular deli customers about my recent diagnosis, and this customer had told her that his wife had gone through something similar. He recommended I see a doctor in Boston who, according to him, put a whole team of specialists together for his wife instead of sending her to multiple different specialists.

The idea of going to only one hospital where I would undergo all the necessary tests was appealing to me—at least more so than being shuffled from hospital to hospital and clinic to clinic. So, I told Alex about it, and he reassured me he was going to get in touch with him as soon as possible.

"He said he can see us on May 5th," Alex added.

"So quickly?" I said, thinking it was basically a few days away. "That's good."

"Yes, I was relieved when he told me it could be soon," Alex said, turning to look at me. "I know your sister wants to come with you, but I would like to take you also, please."

I said, "I still want and need her there, and you have to respect that."

Alex nodded in agreement.

Then I sat up straight and met his eyes. There was something in there that I hadn't seen in quite some time. There was clarity. Unchallenged clarity. For the past eight months, whenever I looked into his eyes, I saw a wall, a façade of sorts. As if Alex was pretending to be Alex, but it wasn't really the man I had married almost two decades prior. But now, that façade had disappeared, and all that was left was Alex. My Alex.

"I am going to need all the support I can get from you," I said in a thin but firm voice. "It is going to be a tough year, or maybe even longer than that. I can't be worried about anything else but getting myself better, especially after everything I've been through these last eight months."

Alex looked at me and said, "I understand and want to be by your side."

"I would love to have you by my side during this ordeal, but the only way I will allow you to do so is if you promise me that you will not be seeing her anymore."

Remembering what my sister told me about the cancer being on the right side, I knew I had to fix more than just the cancer itself. I had to heal from the emotional wounds that the affair had caused. I had to ask him to do his part.

I kept looking at him, and he never once let go of my gaze.

Without showing any signs of inner conflict, he leaned in closer to me and whispered, "I promise you."

"Good," I said, feeling butterflies flutter around in my stomach as if we were on our first date.

"Mom," Olivia said, coming back into the kitchen, her eyes red with consumed tears. "Can I FaceTime my friends, please?" Her voice was broken with emotion.

I got up, walked closer to her, and kissed her forehead. Then I said, "Of course. We will need all the support we can get to make it through this."

Bella and Julia soon walked into the kitchen and asked if they, too, could get in touch with their friends and share the news. Alex and I agreed to let them. Before I knew it, my friend Tamara had gathered a bunch of Bella's soccer friends and drove them over to comfort her.

> My command is this: Love each other as I have loved you. Greater love has no one than this: to lay down one's life for one's friends. (John 15:12-13)

I looked around the kitchen and was met with flashbacks of past conversations held there. Too many tears had been shed in that kitchen. Too many certainties had faded into oblivion there. Too many fake smiles had been forced around that table. This emotional rip current had the potential of dragging us all into the water, never to resurface again. I had to put a stop to it. It was time for a change.

"I want to sell this house," I said to Alex all in one breath.

"What?" Alex looked at me with furrowed brows. "Why?"

"I don't want to live here anymore," I said. "Too many bad memories are floating around. I can sense it. It's not good for the girls or me. We need a fresh start."

"Alright," Alex said without putting up a fight. In fact, his tone conveyed an understanding. Perhaps he, too, wanted a fresh start. "I'll help you look for a new house."

"I don't want a house," I said, looking at him. "This is a house, and I want to sell it."

Alex tilted his head in confusion.

"I need a home," I explained, holding my hands together in a prayer position.

I don't want a house. I need a home.

"I'll help you find a home for you and the girls," he said, wrapping his hands around mine.

☩

A few days later, Alex, my sister, and I went to Boston to meet with the doctor. On the way there, I was worried about Alex and my sister spending time together because his affair had broken her heart too. She was only nine years old when Alex and I started dating, and she looked up to him like a little sister looks up to an older brother.

However, I was relieved to see that the two of them were cordial with each other. I knew my sister had done a lot of work to bring herself to forgive him, especially because she knew that Alex would be her partner to help me recover.

Once at the doctor's, his assistant ushered me into a hospital room where I met with many different specialists. One by one, they came in and talked to me about my diagnosis, ran tests, and reassured me that I was in good hands.

I felt like I was. Sure, this was not the scenario I ever wanted to be in, but if I had to be in it, then I was content with being surrounded by people who showed genuine care for me. Every doctor I met sat down next to me, and judging by the type of questions they asked, they were interested not just in my medical history but in my mental health, hobbies, hopes, and dreams. They made me feel like I was not just a patient but a real human being. And for that, I was thankful.

Meanwhile, both Alex and my sister sat in the room with me. They took turns bringing me snacks and drinks, asking me if I needed anything, and updating me on how the girls were doing back home, where they stayed in the company of my parents and Alex's parents.

As the day came to an end, the doctor called us into his office. Alex, my sister, and I sat down next to each other, the doctor behind his desk. After going through the many details of the plan of action he and his team had put together for my specific case, he announced, "Surgery Day will be June 8th."

"Oh, that's good," Alex said. "That's sooner than we expected, right?" He turned to look at me.

"I can't do it on that day," I said, looking at the doctor but feeling Alex's gaze. "It'll be the same day that Olivia graduates eighth grade." Then, I turned to Alex and explained, "I have, no, *we* have already put them through so much this past year. The girls—and Olivia in particular—deserve to graduate eighth grade with her mother standing there, not laying in a hospital bed hooked up to a million machines."

For a moment, nobody said anything.

For a moment, reality was too heavy to shoulder.

Then, the doctor intervened. "That's not a problem," he said, looking through his online calendar. "We can move it to July 6th."

"Can't we do it before then?" Alex asked the doctor.

"I'm afraid that's the earliest we have after June 8th," the doctor said.

"No problem," I said. "July 6th works, thank you."

Then, after going through some paperwork for the upcoming surgery, it was finally time to leave.

Alex, my sister, and I walked to his car, which was parked nearby. Sitting in the passenger seat, I looked in the rearview mirror and saw the hospital becoming smaller and smaller as Alex drove us away from it.

"Are you okay?" he asked me.

I took a deep breath, closed my eyes, and prayed a silent prayer.

God, I need you to hold my hand and give foresight, courage, and sharpness to the doctors who are going to take care of me. Guide them through what we are all about to go through, enlighten their path, and talk to their hearts as they make important decisions. But most of all, keep my family safe. My life is in your hands. I trust you.

God, my life is in your hands. A numbing sensation rushed through my body and made me feel as if I was weightless, as if flying high above, passing all the clouds, and surrounded by the purest and clearest blue skies. My lungs were free to breathe, taking in all the clean air that effortlessly flowed inside me, purifying my body and soul.

I smiled and opened my eyes.

Then, turning to look at Alex, I said, "Yes, I believe I am."

Chapter Sixteen

"Read this while I'm in surgery today," I whispered to Julia, handing her a letter I had written. It was 4:30 a.m., and I could see my two other daughters were still sleeping—the girls and I shared a hotel room adjacent to my sister, brother-in-law, and nephew, an unlocked door separating both of our rooms. My parents' room was just down the hallway.

I couldn't wait for the other two girls to wake up, though, because I was about to leave the hotel and head to the hospital, as the medical team expected me to check in at five o'clock. As she took the letter, she glanced at the others I had with me: one for Olivia, one for Bella, one for my sister, one for my parents, and one for Alex.

A week prior, I had told Alex I didn't need him to come to Boston because my parents and sister were driving down with me, to which he replied, "Fine, but I'm coming anyway."

The funny thing was that I didn't even tell him at which hotel I was going to stay, nor did he tell me which hotel he had booked for himself. Once we were both in Boston, we realized that we had booked hotels in front of each other, making it easy for Alex to come and check on all of us, as it was just a short walk away.

"Can you also put these letters on the desk so they can read them when they wake up?" I asked Julia as I gave her the letters I had written for her sisters. "And this one to your father?" I handed her Alex's as well. "He'll be here later to get you girls to breakfast."

Julia nodded, her eyes puffy with lack of sleep and apprehension for what that day represented.

I kissed her and the sleeping girls goodbye, reassured her I was in great hands and had nothing to worry about, and then took the calming pill the doctors had given me. Then, my parents and sister accompanied me to check in since Alex had to take care of the girls.

The moment I stepped foot into the hospital, I felt a knot in my throat and knew exactly what it was: fear of the unknown, unshed tears, and the realization of mortality. Since the diagnosis, I had done my best to put up a façade and pretend like it wasn't that big of a deal when I was around my girls. But deep inside, I was shattered into a million pieces.

There were moments when I felt like my body had betrayed me; there were moments when I asked myself if I was going to see all three of my girls graduate from high school; there were moments when I looked up to the sky and felt the urge to yell, why me?

Deep inside, I was shattered into a million pieces.

I took a deep breath and swallowed, forcing that knot down to the pit of my stomach. It wasn't the time to deal with unresolved emotions. It was time to face reality. It was time to undergo breast cancer surgery. Luckily, the calming pill took effect as I waved goodbye to my parents.

The nurses let my sister help me get changed into a hospital gown before I was wheeled into the operating room, my bed carried by strangers wearing white coats. I looked up, and all I saw were sterile white walls and long ceiling lamps. I couldn't help but wonder how many people these lights and walls witnessed slide by every single day.

My eyes closed as I entered the operating room. When I woke up, I was back in my hospital room, and judging by the lack of pain, I imagine the doctors had me on strong painkillers that did exactly what they were supposed to do.

However, I couldn't say the same for the rest of my family members who had accompanied me to Boston. Soon after I opened my eyes, my sister, who was in the room with me, told me that our mother was in the emergency room of the same hospital because of severe back pain—she had hurt her back two weeks prior after taking a misstep, though my sister told me she knew it was a way for her body to manifest her refusal of my cancer diagnosis.

"Is she going to be okay?" I asked her, my voice groggy from the deep sleep I had just woken up from.

"Yeah, she'll be fine," she said, walking closer to me and removing my hair from my forehead. "But doctors think she'll need surgery soon."

"Ugh," I said, clearing my throat in an attempt to regain my normal tone. "I am so sorry. When it rains, it pours, huh?"

"I guess so," she said. "But don't worry about her now, okay? I want you to focus on yourself. The doctors down at the ER are taking good care of Mom, and I'll go check on her soon, so I'll be able to give you an update."

"Thank you," I said.

I looked around the room, which was bare and sterile as any other hospital room. There were two chairs and a small coffee table in the corner, right in front of my bed. To my right, a large window overlooked the hospital parking lot. So it wasn't the most glamorous view, but it still provided all the necessary sunlight.

Then, the door opened slightly, and Alex walked in, almost tiptoeing.

"Oh, hi," he said. "You're awake." There was a genuine smile on his face, one that prompted me to smile at him in return. After greeting my sister, he asked me, "How are you feeling?"

"Okay, for now," I said, watching him walk closer to me.

"Are you in any pain?" he asked.

"Not at the moment," I reassured him.

"I'm glad to hear that," Alex said, placing a cup on the nightstand next to me. "I brought you a hot tea in case you felt like it."

"Thank you. That was thoughtful of you."

"Is there anything else you need that I can get for you?" he asked, looking at me with such gentle eyes, something he hadn't done in so long that it gave me butterflies.

"No, thank you," I said. "I am going to try to get some rest now."

"Okay," my sister said. "We'll let you rest then."

"Of course," Alex replied softly, then he leaned over and kissed my forehead. "I'll go tell the girls how you're doing and will see you later when you wake up."

"Okay, tell them I love them," I said. Then, turning to my sister, I added, "Please go check on Mom."

"Will do," she replied. "You just rest now."

I watched them walk out of the room, and once the door closed behind them, I closed my eyes and fell asleep.

✝

I opened my eyes and realized it was still sunny outside.

I guess I didn't sleep that long, I thought to myself. I blinked a few times to allow my eyes to adjust to the bright light that bounced off the white walls of my hospital room and saw my sister sitting at the small coffee table.

"Hi," I said, my voice groggy still.

"Hey," she said, standing up and walking closer to me. "How are you?"

"I'm okay," I said. "How are the girls?"

"They're doing well with Alex and his sisters in the waiting room," she said.

"What are you drinking?" I asked my sister, who was sipping from a paper cup with a plastic lid.

"Turmeric latte. I walked all over Boston trying to find one for us," she said, taking another sip.

She handed me my beverage, and as I lifted my head from my pillow to grab my cup, I suddenly remembered that I was hooked up to all sorts of machines when I felt a tube pulling me back down.

"Let me just put it here," she said, placing the cup on my nightstand.

But when the aroma rose from the cup and reached my nose, I gasped. "There's coffee in it!" I said out loud.

My sister believed in clean eating, holistic remedies, and living a balanced lifestyle. She did not drink coffee and hadn't had any in many, many years because she was highly

167

sensitive to caffeine. I knew that if she kept drinking it, her body would have a bad reaction to it.

"What?" she said, frowning. "No, it's just turmeric and almond milk." She dismissed me with a hand gesture, probably thinking I didn't know what I was talking about because of all the drugs running through my system.

There have been many times in my life when I was wrong. This was not one of them. Soon after she finished her "turmeric latte," my sister began shaking, trembling, and breathing intensely. Her behavior was erratic, too, as she started spilling out everything that she must have been keeping inside of her: my diagnosis and surgery, Mom's back problems, and so much more—which was why she didn't realize what she had actually been drinking. She was having a panic attack, and a severe one at that. Not long after, she ended up in the emergency room, not to check up on our mother as she told me she would but as a patient herself.

All I could think of was, thank goodness Alex and both my sisters-in-law were there to help with the girls.

✝

The day after surgery, the hospital discharged me. Alex took me back to my hotel room, where my mom and sister were also recovering from their own emergencies. We have a picture of all of us with our hospital bracelets on to commemorate the moment. The next day, my sister drove my parents and me back home, and Alex took the girls to his house. After dropping my parents off at their house, my sister took me back to mine. Once we arrived, I found a surprise waiting for me on my doorstep.

"What's that?" I asked my sister, who had decided to stay over at my house to make sure I was recovering well.

She shrugged and brought the package inside the house for me.

"It's from Alex," she said, looking at the sender's information.

"Oh?" I walked closer to the package and waited for her to open it. When she did, I couldn't believe my eyes. "Oh my God," I said, placing both hands over my mouth.

"Wow, it's beautiful," my sister said, lifting the sculpture from the box.

It was a David Kracov sculpture titled *Book of Life*, made of an open book with over two-thousand colorful butterflies flying out of it. Each butterfly represents a child who escaped the Chornobyl catastrophe, while poems written by children killed at Auschwitz filled the pages.

"It's been years," I said, genuinely surprised by his gesture. "I can't believe he remembered."

"What?" my sister asked.

"Alex and I first saw this in Key West many years ago while we were on vacation," I explained. "And it immediately caught my eye for how gorgeous it is. Then, when I learned the meaning behind it, I fell in love with it." I walked closer to it to admire each hand-painted metal butterfly. "Then I saw it once again in a house that I was viewing to potentially buy . . . and I remember telling him that I saw this sculpture again and how beautiful it was."

"What do you think it means?" my sister asked. "Do you think this is a message that Alex is trying to send you?"

"I don't know," I whispered, suddenly feeling like I was the one with butterflies in my stomach. "Whatever his reason was, I am glad Alex did."

"You should call him and thank him for his gesture," my sister said.

"I will," I said, smiling at her.

Later that evening, I called Alex and told him I had found his surprise.

"I'm glad it made you smile," he said.

"Yes! I can't believe you remembered. Thank you," I said, still smiling from his gift. "Where did you find it?"

"I did some research, and when I finally found it, I knew that it belonged in our . . . *your* house," he said, catching his own mistake.

"Well," I said with a smile, "thank you again. It means a lot."

And we wished each other a good night.

When the girls came back from Alex's house, they were just as in awe of Alex's gift as I was, making his gesture even more special to me. Since they didn't know about the history behind the sculpture and why it was so special to me, I took the occasion to share that with them. I could tell by the sparkle in their eyes and the big smile on their faces that they loved the sculpture as much as I did.

I started to realize that something about Alex was different and had been for some time. Every day after my surgery, he checked on me and my recovery progress, even though my sister never left my side. Thank goodness she didn't because a week after surgery, I woke up to a horrifying sight: my left breast was purple!

I yelled for her, and she rushed to my room right away.

"Why is this happening?" I asked her, my breathing becoming increasingly more intense with fear. Fortunately, the girls were at Alex's, or else they would have been traumatized by what I saw.

"I don't know. Let me take photos and send them to the doctor in Boston," she said, holding her phone as steady as she could.

The doctor on call was quick to tell my sister she had to bring me to Boston immediately. So I got up, got dressed, and a few minutes later, we were both in her car. We had barely backed out of the driveway when my sister glanced at the drains the surgeons placed in my breasts and yelled, "They're about to overflow!"

I looked down and gasped in shock at what I saw: my breast was purple, and both drains were almost completely full.

"I just emptied them," she said. "I'm afraid you're going to bleed out. We have to get to the closest emergency room. You're in no condition to take on a three-hour drive to Boston."

I nodded, grateful she was there with me, but once again, feeling that knot in my throat.

Once at the emergency room, they admitted me right away. After running multiple tests that kept me in the hospital for ten hours, the medical staff assisting me decided it was best if they took me to Boston via ambulance. So, my sister and I got into the ambulance and went to Boston, in what was a long and uncomfortable drive—though I don't remember most of it because they had given me drugs to make me sleep and remain calm.

Meanwhile, my sister called Alex to update him on what was happening and arranged for the girls to stay with my parents—even though my mom was still dealing with severe back issues, for which she had surgery scheduled in the next few weeks.

As soon as we arrived at the hospital, they wheeled me to a room, and, much to my surprise, I found Alex standing there, which was a big—and nice—surprise.

"I brought you some food," he said, coming closer to the bed. "Salmon filet and salad."

I could have cried over how happy that gesture had made me. I had been starving all day because the doctors wouldn't let me eat—they were scared that I needed to undergo emergency surgery, and, given that I would have to have anesthesia, I couldn't eat. But besides my hunger, what almost brought me to tears was that Alex thought I could have been hungry and had gone out of his way to ensure I had a healthy, delicious meal to look forward to. He hadn't done that in such a long time.

"Thank you," I said, emotion wavering in my voice.

"Of course," Alex said. "I came here as soon as I heard and got myself a room at the hotel connected to the hospital."

"Okay," I said, finally enjoying a warm meal. "They said they want to keep me here for a couple of days under observation to see if there is another hematoma."

"I can stay here as long as needed," he reassured me.

During the next few days, doctors and nurses came and went, checking my scars, measuring the amount of blood in my drains, and everything else in between.

"Everything seems to be okay," I reassured my sister on the third day we were there. "I don't think I need surgery. Why don't you go back home? I'm sure the baby needs you more than me."

"Are you sure?" she said. "I don't mind staying. You know that."

"I know, but Alex is here, and from what I've heard the doctors say, they might discharge me tomorrow," I said.

"So unless you want Alex to drive you back home, I would suggest taking the train back today."

"Nah," she said with a smile. "I think I'll stay here. I'd feel better if I stayed."

"Okay," I said.

But a few hours later, my sister was on the train back to New York. When she called me from her house, I asked her what made her change her mind.

"I have no idea," she said. "It was the weirdest thing. I felt like somebody picked me up from your hospital room and put me on that train. I know it sounds crazy, but that's the best way I can describe it."

"Oh, wow," I said. "That is crazy." Although, it wasn't that crazy to me. I knew God's hand had played a big role in this instance, somehow convincing my sister to leave me with Alex. After all, I had prayed for God to help me through this ordeal, and I guess one of the many ways He answered my prayer was to allow Alex and me to be alone.

"How are you feeling, anyway?" she asked.

"I'm still in pain, but the doctors said they are indeed discharging me tomorrow morning, so I guess I'm coming home tomorrow."

I knew God's hand had played a big role.

"That's good," she said. "Call me tomorrow then."

"Yes, I will call you tomorrow."

As I hung up, Alex walked into the room with dinner, which we enjoyed together as we talked about nothing in particular.

The following morning, after Alex and I had breakfast, he went downstairs to pick up a wheelchair to help me get out of the hospital. While he was gone, I was already ready to leave the room because I had received my discharge papers. But when I got up, my left breast suddenly became painful and got bigger and bigger. It was as if somebody had placed a balloon in it and kept adding air.

I gasped and quickly pushed the call button on the remote attached to my hospital bed. After the nurse checked what was happening to my chest, doctors came into the room and told me I needed to undergo emergency surgery.

"What?" I said out loud. "But I just had breakfast!"

"We can wait six hours for the surgery, but we can't let you leave the hospital," one of the doctors said. "We have to remove the blood clot."

"Alright, ready to—" Alex stopped talking the moment he entered the room with the wheelchair and saw the nurses and doctors reattaching me to all kinds of machines. "What's going on?"

I updated him on what happened while he was downstairs, and his jaw dropped in shock. He started crying, scared of my drains overflowing again and not knowing what was happening to me.

Later that day, I underwent another surgery—this one way more painful than the first one. When I was wheeled back to the room, I saw Alex and his sisters, who must have driven there to keep him company.

My sisters-in-law asked me how I felt, but I couldn't really talk because I was groggy and in pain, with tubes and drains still sticking out of me. All I could do was wonder if this nightmare was ever going to end.

God, please help me understand why this is all happening to me. I prayed silently as tears slowly left my closed eyes and traveled hopelessly down my cheeks. *Why are you making me go through all of this?*

God, please help me understand why this is happening to me.

What am I supposed to learn from this lesson? Eventually, I fell asleep praying.

The next day, my body seemed to be recovering well, and I felt much better. Though I still had pain, it wasn't as strong as what I had experienced the previous days. So, I decided to take my phone, which had been sitting on the nightstand next to my bed, and scroll through Facebook.

"What?" I said with a gasp.

"What?" Alex echoed. He was sitting in an armchair that doubled as a pullout bed but got up to check on what had shocked me so much.

"You bought a house?" I asked him, showing him the post our realtor had left on his Facebook page, and that, as a consequence, appeared on my feed. It was accompanied by a caption that read: "Congratulations to Alex for buying the house!"

I felt tears rush to my eyes. Did Alex buy a house without me? Yes, I told him I wanted to move out of the house the girls and I currently lived in, and he did offer to help me look for one, but why go behind my back and buy a house for himself and the girls when he didn't even tell me he was looking for one? Having to find out through social media felt like a huge slap in the face. *This really means that we are getting a divorce and we are no longer a family,* I thought.

Alex had an unusual smile on his face as he sat beside me and placed my phone on the nightstand. Then, he embraced my hands with his, leaned closer to me, and said, "I bought the house for *us*."

Us?

He said us?

There hadn't been an us in almost a year. My heart was beating a million miles an hour. Could this be true?

I remained unmoving as I stared at Alex, unable to form words.

Was this really happening?

Then, Alex looked me deeper in the eyes and whispered, "What do you say? Shall we try again?"

This was the moment when I knew that God had a plan for us all along. Every piece was falling right into place. It all made sense now: my diagnosis and blood clot, my mom's back injury, and my sister's panic attack, which forced her to leave me in the hospital alone with Alex, allowing us to have time to ourselves. I also knew that God's timing about Alex's affair was perfect. This cancer had been unknowingly growing in me. Had I not found out about it when I did, had I not quickly lost a lot of weight, I might have never discovered my tumor.

This was the moment when I knew that God had a plan for us all along.

My prayers had been answered.

Epilogue

"Mom, we need to go shopping for prom tomorrow!" Olivia said as she walked into the living room where Alex and I had been watching a movie together.

"Sounds good," I answered with a smile and then watched her walk toward her bedroom.

Alex squeezed my hand and looked at me. Then he whispered, "Can you believe we are going to be empty nesters soon?"

My heart skipped a beat at the sounds of those words.

He was right. Julia and Bella were already in college, and Olivia was going to be on her way in a few short months.

I released a heavy sigh. Was it relief? Maybe. Was it sadness? Probably. Whatever it was, the reality was that all three of our daughters had grown up to be loving, caring, determined young women who were ready to take on the world. And as a parent, I couldn't have been prouder of them.

"We've made it," I said to Alex, squeezing his hand in return.

"It's going to be just you and me from now on," he said. The movie playing became background noise. "And you know what that means?"

"What?" I asked, knowing what he was going to say because it was something we had been planning since the girls were little. But I just wanted to hear him say it again.

"We are going to have so much fun!" he said, laughing. "We are going to travel the world, go out for romantic dinners, enjoy this big house all to ourselves, and of course, keep going to therapy."

A sense of peace blanketed me as my chest felt light as ever.

We've really made it, I thought, as Alex focused back on the movie.

Four years prior, this reality seemed to be slipping out of my hands and sinking into the abyss of absolute devastation to never reemerge again. The affair almost destroyed us. The cancer and affair almost destroyed me. But with God's help and guidance, lots of hard work, and dedication to one another, Alex and I survived it all.

With God's help and guidance, lots of hard work, and dedication to one another, we survived.

At that moment, sitting on the couch with my husband and dreaming of our future, I was flooded with memories of that fateful day at the hospital where he asked me to get back together, a question I happily—yet cautiously—said yes to.

Soon after I recovered from the post-surgery setback, Alex and I bought a house together. Not the one he had put an offer on and that I found out about via Facebook.

We ended up choosing another one because that one house and its neighborhood did not have sidewalks—a must for me as I have always enjoyed going for long walks.

Though it was hard to move during chemotherapy and radiation—the side effects were exhausting and debilitating—the girls, my family, and Alex never once made me feel alone or overwhelmed. After seven months of treatments, I received a clean bill of health, one that I have kept up with ever since.

Alex and I also decided we needed to go to couples therapy to truly work on ourselves if we wanted our marriage to succeed. Though not every session was easy to handle because of topics that came up during our conversations, we both knew that we had to do the hard work to move forward and heal. Session after session, we learned more about one another, how we showed love for each other, and what we recognized as validation and understanding. We talked, but most of all, we listened to each other, and that made all the difference in the world.

"What's on your mind?" Alex asked me, bringing me back to the present while the closing credits scrolled on the TV.

"Oh," I said, closing my eyes for a moment and clearing my throat. "How the girls reacted when we told them we were getting back together."

"Oh yes," he said, laughing. "They were like, *Duh!*"

"Yes, they knew it was coming," I said, smiling at their nonchalant reaction.

"But remember how they were also disappointed?" Alex said with a smile, adjusting himself on the couch, placing one arm behind my back.

"Oh my gosh, yes! They had become so good at getting what they wanted from one of us when the other said no,"

I said, shaking my head. "Not that things have changed much now."

"Our three girls are something else," Alex said, a sweet tone in his voice. "We've raised really good kids."

I nodded in agreement as I felt my heart heavy with motherly love but also with a sense of loss because the girls were now starting their own lives. Alex must have sensed the clashing emotions within me because he turned the TV off, scooted closer, and whispered, "How about we start planning our first trip together as husband and wife instead of Mom and Dad?"

A smile effortlessly formed on my face.

"Where can we go?" I asked.

"Wherever you want," he said.

And just like that, our future began.

Oh, taste and see that the Lord is good;
blessed is the man who trusts in Him!

—Psalm 34:8

Acknowledgments

I have to start by thanking my husband: my world, my love. We have been through it all—extreme highs and extreme lows—but there is no one else I would do this life with. I could not have undertaken this journey without you. Thank you for letting me tell our story; it couldn't have been easy for you. I would do it all over again with you. Thank you for being the strong man of God that you are and for everything you do for me and the girls. I love you more.

My girls, Julia, Isabella, and Olivia: Dad and I tell everyone we know how amazing you are. For three girls so close in age, you never gave us any problems, and you have all grown into intelligent, kind, beautiful young women. I can't wait to see what the future holds for you. You girls have been through a lot, and I am proud of the way you handled it. Dad and I love you more than you will ever know.

I will forever be indebted to the best younger sister, Elaina. You read every word of every draft of this book, and your input was always better than anything I could have thought of. You saved my life more than once with your knowledge of naturopathic doctors I should see, foods and supplements I should be on, keeping track of my drains, and getting me to a hospital before I was in real trouble. You know my medical history better than I do, and the time you took away from Vinny and Vincent while I was going through everything will never be forgotten. Thank you for being you and throwing the best, most epic Boob-Voyage party ever! I'm glad I asked Mom and Dad for you. I love you.

I am extremely grateful to my hard-working, loving parents. I always knew you believed in me and wanted the best for me. Thank you for being adamant about me going to college and for teaching me that my job in life was to learn, be happy, and know and understand myself. What you didn't know was all the times I was trying to be strong in front of you, I was falling apart inside. Thank you for being stronger than I was when I needed you most. Oh, and I am sorry for telling you I had cancer in the middle of lunch hour at the deli. My bad! I love you.

To my mother-in-law, Lucia, and my sisters-in-law, Marilena and Cristina: We had a rough little patch there for a bit, but thank you for always treating me like a daughter and a sister. So blessed to have grown up with you and to know how fiercely you protect your family. I love you all.

To Monica, Lori, Maureen, Diane, Louisa, Claudia, Tamara, and Denyse: You ladies are the best! The meal trains you set up, the lunches, calls, texts, prayers, dinners you took me out to so I would get out of the house, and most importantly, the TEQUILA SHOTS!! Thank you ladies for your friendship. I love each and every one of you.

The Cape Cod crew, Laurie, Bill, Dave, Nancy, Pete & Vicki, Paul & Gwen: I loved loved loved our week in the cape every year. Some of my best memories are with you all. Ten adults and thirteen girls in one house?! Were we crazy? Somehow, together we made it all work, and I will treasure those days for as long as I live. Love you guys.

Paul and Gwen: Where do I start with you two? I don't know how you did it. How did you actually go to work or get anything done? The amount of text messages and calls I sent you in those eight months probably broke a world record. Thank you both for being there every minute of the day and night for my rants and cries. You have seen me at my absolute lowest and literally lifted me up. Thank you for bringing me back to church. That first day, I sat in the parking lot crying so bad I didn't think I could walk into church, but your words were, "That just means this is where you should be," and you were right. I'll always remember that. You both are very special to us, and I thank God you are in our lives. Love you.

Pam, Cathy and Missy: Thank you for our monthly lunches and breakfasts. I needed those more than you know. Your wisdom, prayers, and friendship mean the world to me. We are survivors!

My Nanni: I am so blessed you are here to guide me with your wisdom. At 90 years old, you are still holding everyone and everything together. I love you so much!

Aunt Maria, Uncle Louie, Uncle Mico: You guys are like siblings to me. Thank you for the food and keeping me fed. Seriously, where did you all learn how to cook? I am so grateful that we are so close, and I can call you guys for anything.

Brunella Costagliola: You took my story and gave it life. Thank you for the countless hours on the phone and listening to every detail of my journey.

About Gina Tronco

Faith and family are the most important things to Gina Tronco. Music and helping people have been integral to her life from a young age, so it was natural for Gina to earn a Master of Science degree from The College of St. Rose and become a music teacher. Soon after marrying her husband, Alessandro, she transitioned to being a stay home mom to their three children. That role is her proudest achievement and divine purpose in life.

After receiving a cancer diagnosis at the age of forty-two, Gina found herself even more immersed in her faith and being of service to others who have also been diagnosed.

Every community she's contributed to knows her for her inspirational message and love for people. She has participated in various charity events and is always ready and willing to help someone going through health or marital circumstances. Gina has truly turned her mess into her message.

Gina resides in Albany with her husband, Alessandro, and their dogs, Leo and Knox. They have three incredible daughters pursuing big dreams.

Connect with Gina at WhyIsThisHappening.net

GINA WANTS TO CONNECT WITH YOU

Is your world falling apart?
Gina can help.
Follow her on your favorite
social media platforms.

WHYISTHISHAPPENING.NET

About Alessandro Tronco

Gina's childhood sweetheart became her husband. Together with Alessandro, the couple decided to lift up others with their stories. Alessandro's book, *The Buddha Who Drove a Bentley*, inspires others to make the necessary changes to live their most authentic life, find true happiness, and have it all.

**What if you could gain the whole world,
but it would cost your soul?**

Most people think Vincent, a man in his late forties, has truly arrived. From the outside, he has it all: money, an affluent lifestyle, a great family, a lucrative career, and impeccable health. But on the inside, he knows the truth. The weight of wearing this mask has taken a toll on his soul.

Just living a day in his own skin is a price he's unsure he wants to pay. In a moment of desperation, Vincent escapes in his Bentley and heads to the mountains. While driving on the windy roads, he recalls painful memories, moments of betrayal, and toxic lies. Alone and overwhelmed, he wakes up in an exotic and unfamiliar place.

On his journey, he meets unexpected guides. Each one teaches Vincent an essential lesson that begins to heal the pain. Some include how you must:

- Forgive yourself before you can forgive others
- Tell yourself the truth, no matter what the cost
- Slow down, or you will miss the most magical moments
- Stay connected and believe your life is part of a bigger story

Through these chance encounters, Vincent begins to rediscover his lost soul. He's confronted with a choice that has eternal implications. Does he stay in this otherworldly place or return to his former life in hopes of changing the world?

The Buddha Who Drove a Bentley will help you on your own journey to live your most authentic life, find true happiness, and have it all.

Discover more at TheBuddhaWhoDroveABentley.com

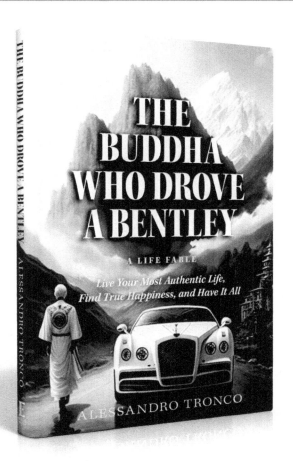

About Spirit Water

Gina and her husband, Alessandro, are very health-conscious and environmentally aware. In an effort to promote this lifestyle worldwide, they partnered with others to create Spirit Water, a flavored water company that focuses on uplifting souls and saving the planet.

Spirit is a company that envisions a world where everyone is healthy and thriving, and every sip of our flavored water is a step toward a better future. Good health and a better world go hand in hand, and we are committed to using our flavored water products to promote both.

We use only the finest, all-natural ingredients in sustainable packaging and support initiatives promoting health, wellness, and sustainability. With every sip of Spirit Water, we encourage people to embrace a healthier, more conscious way of living and to join us in creating a brighter future for all.

Discover more at SpiritWaterInc.com

EVERY SIP OF OUR FLAVORED WATER IS A STEP TOWARD A BETTER FUTURE. WE BELIEVE THAT GOOD HEALTH AND A BETTER WORLD GO HAND IN HAND

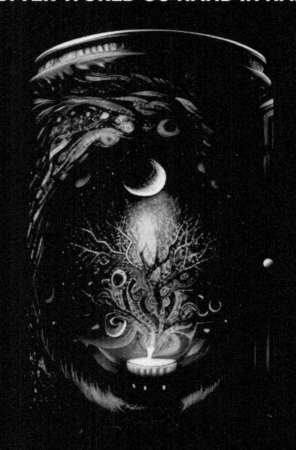

SPIRITWATERINC.COM

THIS BOOK IS PROTECTED INTELLECTUAL PROPERTY

The author of this book values Intellectual Property. The book you just read is protected by Easy IP™, a proprietary process, which integrates blockchain technology giving Intellectual Property "Global Protection." By creating a "Time-Stamped" smart contract that can never be tampered with or changed, we establish "First Use" that tracks back to the author.

Easy IP™ functions much like a Pre-Patent™ since it provides an immutable "First Use" of the Intellectual Property. This is achieved through our proprietary process of leveraging blockchain technology and smart contracts. As a result, proving "First Use" is simple through a global and verifiable smart contract. By protecting intellectual property with blockchain technology and smart contracts, we establish a "First to File" event.

Powered By Easy IP™

LEARN MORE AT EASYIP.TODAY

Made in United States
North Haven, CT
08 March 2024

49695641R00117